D1497881

KNIGHTS OF
THE NEW
TECHNOLOGY

David Thomas

Knights of
THE NEW
Technology

The Inside Story
of Canada's
Computer Elite

KEY PORTER·BOOKS

Canadian Cataloguing in Publication Data

Thomas, David, 1947–
   Knights of the new technology

Includes index.
ISBN 0-919493-16-5

1. Computer industry — Canada — Biography.
2. Microelectronics industry — Canada — Biography.
I. Title.

HD9696.C63C38 1983   338.4'762138195'0922   C83-098998-6

Key Porter Books
59 Front Street East
Toronto, Ontario M5E 1B3

Designed by Donald Fernley

This book was typeset from copy supplied by the author from his personal computer in Hudson, P.Q. and telecommunicated to typesetting equipment at Imprint Typesetting, Toronto.

Printed and bound in Canada
by T.H. Best Printing Company Limited

To Aurélie and Evan

CONTENTS

ACKNOWLEDGEMENTS

The subjects of this book must be gratefully recognized for the openness with which they revealed their failures and embarrassments as well as their triumphs. Thanks also to Anne Beirne, who shared in the research, and to the editor, Janet Craig, whom I suspect of benefiting from a secret royalty on the use of commas.

Hudson, Quebec
August 1983

KNIGHTS OF
THE NEW
TECHNOLOGY

The Morning of the New Magicians

SS *Rotterdam* eased slowly from her berth at Fort Lauderdale, the golden rays of the setting sun playing alchemist with her black hull. She turned away from the cascade of streamers and balloons let loose to celebrate her sailing and steamed southeast across the calm surface of the Gulf Stream. Aboard, soothing themselves in the warm evening air wafting gently up from Cuba, were 137 couples and 101 singles selected from the élite of American big business.

They and their fellow guests had been gently shanghaied by the promise of a pampering pleasure cruise to the Bahamas, but the *Rotterdam* was in fact sailing under war rules this November 3, 1982. She had been chartered by Northern Telecom Limited of Canada, and her mission was to declare war the old way, by sailing into the enemy's own harbour with guns trained on the potentate's palace.

The passenger list was drawn from the executive suites of the so-called *Fortune 500*, the annual blue book of corporate power compiled by the magazine that is the *Vogue* of the world of big business. Northern Telecom still treats the *Rotterdam* cruise like a strategic secret and refuses to divulge the names of the 375 passengers aboard for that November cruise. It will reveal only that they included top executives of 154 companies such as General Foods, Citicorp, and Kaiser Aluminum. Northern Telecom's explanation for the secrecy is that the cruise guests might not like the publicity.

A more likely reason may be the entire electronics industry's congenital inability to talk straight. Though the computer and communications sectors enjoy a fashionable new identification as the "information industry," there are few other areas of human endeavour, outside of totalitarian politics, where truth and information are treated so cavalierly. Getting even the most banal corporate information from International Business Machines Corporation is like trying to pry state secrets from the Kremlin. On the other hand, the truth-twisting hype in the industry's business-page advertising of its latest miracle machines finds its match only in the promises of eternal beauty that corrupt the credibility of women's magazines. There is an unintentional honesty in the computer industry's recourse to classic mythologies and science fiction for the names of companies and products. Aside from being the inspirations for names that Canadian electronics entrepreneurs have chosen to identify their businesses or machines, *Nabu, Gandalf, Hyperion, Taurus,* and *Phoenix* share in common the fact that their powers are superhuman – and at the very least exaggerated.

During their three days as cosseted captives aboard the *Rotterdam,* the passengers were treated to a spectacle of fear mongering and promises of salvation reminiscent of a rural revival meeting. Preachings by Northern's own top executives were illumined by fire-and-brimstone displays of sound and light that required nineteen slide projectors. They heard dire warnings of "confusion" and "chaos" threatening their defenceless companies. The villains were the big computer empires out to control the world for their own dark purposes. At that very moment, their corporations were becoming a babel of mechanical diversity as the computer sellers enticed their customers down the slippery slope of incompatibility by tempting them with machines that could speak seductively but in strange tongues understood only by members of their own tribe.

The Prince of Darkness behind this evil of incompatibility was never named. But the IBM logo lurked in everyone's mind like an imagined shark fin slicing hungry circles in the waters around the *Rotterdam.* Nor did Northern Telecom give away its own intelligence on the enemy's designs. Nevertheless, it and telecommunications companies around the world are disturbed by IBM's encircling of the globe with a ring of orbiting computers. Not many weeks before the *Rotterdam* sailed, the space shuttle *Columbia* opened its cargo bay to the black sky and expelled a barrel-shaped copper-coloured satellite. It was the third belonging to Satellite Business Systems, a subsidiary that IBM owns with COMSAT General Corporation and Aetna Life & Casualty, a partnership imposed by an American government leery of

14

allowing IBM sole control over a world communications system. Already, IBM was routing 160,000 of its own intracompany telephone calls via its satellites and was offering low-cost long-distance service to American homes and businesses. It had even recruited the governments of Great Britain and Italy to its telecommunications network. Besides this direct encroachment on telephone company territory, IBM earlier in 1982 had established the IBM Information Network, which intended to communicate the data of American business across the continent.

The reality of a rival world communications network linking rooftop earth stations sends a cold shudder through the lines of the established telephone system, a system upon which Northern Telecom's existence depends. If IBM were to succeed in recruiting the major corporations of the world to its own communications network, that system would be relegated to second-rate chores.

Northern Telecom's executives urged the *Rotterdam's* passengers not to surrender the result of centuries of struggle to give mankind common connections. Northern Telecom would do its part in saving the corporate world from communications catastrophe by tying polyglot computers together through the old familiar reliable telephone lines. Northern's computer switching systems would be able to do the job – a promise the company called "OPEN World."

The words behind the acronym OPEN groan in their agony at being constrained to fit it. They are there, of course, only in case someone might ask. No one seriously believes "Open Protocol Enhanced Network" carries any more meaning than an overturned Scrabble set. What OPEN World does signify is Northern Telecom's wager that Canadian technological and financial strength can mount a strike against IBM's emerging network for human and machine communications, a network that threatens the telephone system's place at the centre of the communications universe. The urgency of a counter-offensive increased in June 1983 when IBM opened a fifth column within the telephone industry itself. The computer maker bought a 20-per-cent share of Rolm Corporation, an important competitor of Northern's in the sale of telephone systems to businesses. It was now evident that IBM intended to bundle complete telephone service in with its computer networks, freezing Northern and other telephone system specialists out of important markets.

The cruise and the OPEN World strategy were the inspiration of

Northern's former vice-president for marketing, Robert Dyer, a forty-year-old electrical engineer turned supersalesman whose enthusiasm seems almost naïve. Paradoxically, in a high-stakes industry where the deck is laced with unpredictable wild cards, a measure of naïvety seems to be an essential ingredient of success. "We believe that OPEN World will clearly position Northern Telecom as the leading manufacturer and provider of systems that transfer and handle information," Dyer declares. "I know that sounds kind of grandiose, but that is really our intent: to provide an information management system, and I stress the word system. It's not just one individual black box doing something – it's a system of black boxes that can work together with our own products and those of other manufacturers as well." Dyer moved in 1983 from Mississauga to Dallas to take charge of Northern's development of a family of computer terminals and work stations – a direct incursion into the fief of the computer companies.

Like most announcements in the madhouse marketplace of high technology, Northern's promise of an OPEN World was made well before it could deliver the black boxes, the high-tech engineer's designation of his raw inventions before they have been packaged prettily for sale as miracle machines. Dyer and the other Northern Telecom strategists assured the *Rotterdam*'s passengers that the company would commit $1.2 billion toward making the effective connections between computers and the telephone system. At risk is Northern's future as a high-technology multinational. Also at stake is Canada's tradition as a pioneer in communications technology. Will that leadership transcend the confluence of computers and communications or fade into mere folkloric significance like China's invention of gunpowder?

Much of Northern Telecom's war will be fought with salvos of information fired at people like those on the *Rotterdam*'s passenger list. For this, the company is well armed. It takes flair, after all, to charter a cruise ship for a high-tech Tupperware party.

Northern also proved its mastery of information control in the early weeks of 1980 when it managed to spirit its entire Canadian and world headquarters away from a high-rise office tower on Dorchester Boulevard in Montreal without attracting any attention. Northern's headquarters reappeared in a discreet six-storey structure west of Toronto in a synthetic city called Mississauga, where apartment blocks, shopping centres, broadcast radio transmitters, and office buildings take shape across a plain of dead farm land like jungle fungi feeding on a fallen tree. In Mississauga, Italian, not French, is the second language and no one doubts the excellence of industrial growth. Mississauga is reassuringly dull. "The most exciting thing around here is $1.44 Day at Woolco," notes one of Northern's head-office employees.

Northern moved its headquarters staff of two hundred to escape the insistence of the Parti Québécois that French become the domi-nant language of work and the uncertain political future of the province on the eve of the independence referendum in May 1980. Sun Life Assurance Company of Canada had made itself everybody's whipping-boy, resented by secessionists and federalists alike, when it announced a year earlier that it was quitting Quebec for the surer political climate of Ontario. Northern Telecom did not make that mistake. Quietly, it loaded its precious corporate data into trucks parked out of sight behind the building and simply made the move without announcing it. It still hasn't. The transfer was acknowledged only by the appearance of a new corporate address in the fine print of the company's annual report. Even into 1983, Toronto's *Globe and Mail* blithely persisted, in its business pages, in referring to the company as Northern Telecom "of Montreal."

Northern is counting on American Telephone and Telegraph Cor-poration to join in an eventual alliance against the IBM axis, but AT&T is, for the time being, preoccupied by internal upheavals as it divests itself of local Bell telephone companies to keep its promise to the U.S. government. For the first critical years of conflict, Northern Telecom will have to fight on with only limited American assistance.

Victory will mean survival of the company, and also of Canada as a wellspring of high-technology invention. Defeat might mean loss of the principal source of strength and renewal for most of the country's high-technology industry, which, one way or another, is tied like the tail of a kite to the telephone system. The individual elements, whether they are called Mitel, Anik, or most of the dozen other names synonymous with high-tech adventure, can trace their ances-try to the use of telephone technology to defeat distance in a country whose geography defies easy nationhood.

Early in its industrial history, Canada – more precisely, immigrants to Canada – showed a proclivity to dream big dreams. Geographic obstacles were usually the inspiration and the defeat of distance the immediate challenge. The frontier of technology in the 1870s was in the building of transcontinental railways, and nowhere did that require more innovation, daring, and engineering brilliance than in Canada.

It was a Scottish immigrant of 1845 named Sandford Fleming who conceived the Canadian Pacific Railway. Fleming's trek across prairie and mountain in 1872 to seek a pathway for the line demonstrated the physical power and determination of the bearded, burly engineer. Less chronicled is his higher understanding of the essence of communications as the lubricant of human interaction. During the building of the CPR, of which Fleming was chief engineer, every city operated on its own time, based on the sun's passage across the sky. Scheduling trains across this jigsaw puzzle of time zones was a hazardous undertaking, and in 1876 Fleming proposed a global system of twenty-four time zones, each geared to the time maintained by the Royal Observatory, which was then in Greenwich, England. North American railways were quick to seize upon the scheme, and in 1884 the world followed by adopting Fleming's Universal time.

Fleming went on to complete the first electronic communications network to girdle the globe. He engineered and, in 1902, officially opened the British Empire's undersea cable system by sending two telegrams from the Ottawa telegraph office. One followed his railway route west, dipped under the Pacific to cross Asia and Europe, and then dove under the Atlantic to return to Ottawa minutes after it had left. The other travelled the same route but in the opposite direction.

It was also at a place that would become part of Canada that the first transatlantic radio signal was received in 1901. With an antenna hanging from a kite flying over Signal Hill in St. John's, Newfoundland, the Italian electrical engineer and aristocrat Marchese Guglielmo Marconi captured the letter S radioed in Morse code from England. But it was an earlier event, in the year of Marconi's birth, that would be the most profound and long-lasting determinant of Canada's role in connecting citizens and countries.

In July of 1874, at his parents' home in Brantford, Ontario, another immigrant from Scotland named Alexander Graham Bell sketched detailed plans for the telephone. A century later, yet another Canadian of Scottish descent named Marshall McLuhan would help people realize how Bell's invention and the technology that grew directly from it had radically modified human behaviour. "No more unexpected social result of the telephone has been observed," wrote McLuhan in his 1964 book *Understanding Media*, "than its elimination of the red-light district and its creation of the call girl."

Canada's claim to invention of the telephone can be disputed. It was actually two years later in Boston that Bell spilled some acid, and in another room his assistant heard through the experimental telephone the inventor's cry, "Mr. Watson, come here, I want you." On June 25, 1876, the day General George Custer and his troops were annihilated by Sioux Indians at the Little Bighorn, Bell demonstrated his one-way telephone for the first time at the Philadelphia Centennial Exposition. Canada can, however, legitimately boast of the first long-distance telephone call, made when Bell, on August 10, 1876, transmitted a call over wires connecting the Bell family home with the Dominion Telegraph Company office in Brantford and eight miles farther over the telegraph lines to Paris, Ontario. The first telephone lineman was also a Canadian, a farmer named Thomas Brooks who helped Bell rig up stovepipe wire for that first long-distance call.

Bell established his telephone company in Boston in 1877, and he assigned a 75-per-cent interest in the rights to exploit his invention in Canada to his father, Melville. The other 25 per cent went to an American manufacturer called Charles Williams who, in return, was to supply a thousand telephones for installation in Canada. The Bell Telephone Company of Canada had permanent telephone lines in five towns by the end of the year. Its first subscriber was Charles D. Cory of Hamilton, who leased four Bell "Wooden Box Telephones," which looked like shoe boxes with a hole in each end. There was no such thing as a switchboard, and subscribers could call only the other telephone sets that they themselves leased. According to a company advertisement of the day, "Conversation can be easily carried on after slight practice and with the occasional repetition of a word or sentence – after a few trials, the ear becomes accustomed to the peculiar sound."

In 1878, Bell, the inventor, lost control of his business to a group of Boston capitalists. It would not be the last time that a Canadian entrepreneur would lose his company to investors after the utility of his invention had been proven. On the other hand, when his father, Melville Bell, wanted to sell his Canadian telephone rights and move to the States, Canadian investors were either uninterested or could not raise the $100,000 he asked. As a result, the National Bell Telephone Company of Boston acquired them and the American-owned Bell Telephone Company of Canada was chartered by Act of Parliament in 1880. Control of the Canadian company would gradually shift as Canadians bought more and more of its stock.

The world's first factory devoted to the manufacture of telephones was opened in Brantford by James Cowherd. Unfortunately, Cowherd died within months of starting the plant, and Canada was left without a reliable domestic source of telephone equipment. In the United States the situation was different. National Bell controlled its own manufacturing firm, called Western Electric, which became the exclusive and dependable maker of telephone equipment for its American parent. The Canadian subsidiary of National Bell soon followed that example by opening its own manufacturing branch. By 1885 it had grown big enough to be incorporated as a separate company, the Northern Electric and Manufacturing Company.

In 1911, a half interest in Northern Electric was sold to its American cousin Western Electric, which then provided Northern with the best telephone technology of the time. A record in the Bell Canada archives credits Northern with being the world's biggest manufacturer of sleigh bells, but the status of branch plant also gave Northern licence to make gramophones and install Movietone cinema equipment. This included the first "talkie" system in the British Empire at Montreal's Palace Theatre in 1928, five weeks after the release of the first all-talking movie, *Lights of New York*. Despite such dabbles in new technologies, Northern Electric would remain, for half a century, a pale, listless child of the American manufacturer, making Canadian copies of telephone sets and switchboards designed in the United States.

Nobody in Canada seemed to mind the arrangement, but in the United States the Bell system's monopolistic control over the most important telephone companies, long-distance connections, and manufacture of telephone equipment was distrusted. And so, the most important event in the modern history of the Canadian telecommunications industry happened not in Canada but in Washington. In 1956, huge AT&T persuaded the government to suspend an antitrust action against it by agreeing to break Western Electric's stranglehold on the supply of equipment. As part of that so-called consent decree, Western was to stop giving its Canadian subsidiary preferential access to its technical plans. Henceforth, if Northern wanted Western's product designs, it would have to pay the same price for them as any other competitor.

"The consent decree that triggered Northern's change from a dependent company to a world force in telecommunications was an accident which we can look back to and say was the best thing that ever happened to us. But it was an accident that we would never have sought," recalls the man who presided over much of that metamorphosis. Vernon Marquez lives today in retirement on a meadowed estate in an equestrian haven near the village of St-Lazare, west of Montreal. Marquez's wife, Peggy, still rides, but he hasn't mounted a horse since he turned seventy-two in 1981. Instead, he is pursuing plans to market his recent invention which he calls the Petrometer, a sliding scale that converts kilometres per litre into comprehensive miles to the gallon.

Trim, with bearing and visage that might be modelled after those of a British Spitfire pilot, close-trimmed moustache and all, Vernon Marquez could easily pass for a man in his fifties. His voice is rich and tinged with an intriguing aristocratic accent. Sometimes it sounds English, but if you close your eyes and imagine hot sun, the clipped twang of the West Indies echoes through more than half a century of life in Canada. The accent helps Marquez's speech slip easily into earthiness without losing its dignity.

Marquez came to Montreal in 1929 from Trinidad, where his wealthy Portuguese-born father owned a cocoa plantation. Family connections helped him find his first job, soldering wires in Northern Electric's switchboard department at thirty-five cents an hour. Marquez quickly caught the approving eye of management, but when he married in 1933, Marquez resigned. He said he couldn't support a wife on the $24 a week he was then earning and would return with her to live on his father's plantation. The factory manager called him in and asked him how much more would make him stay. Each month throughout Northern's Depression wage cutbacks Marquez received an under-the-table envelope from the boss's office containing an extra $40.95. His privileged climb through the Northern hierarchy culminated with the presidency in 1967 – the company's first chief executive officer who was not an engineer. He was a generalist who had developed a flair and passion for marketing. He was also a maverick among leaders of the country's manufacturing firms, advocating a tough style of international competition for which Canadians were ill prepared.

Marquez now reflects on the curious course of history: "It's fascinating that the antitrust legislation in the United States is presumably designed to be of value to the American people. Yet the paradox is that two of its greatest effects have been of much greater value to the Canadian people: the one that separated Alcan from Alcoa and the one that severed Northern from sucking on the hind teat of Western Electric."

It gradually dawned on Northern and Bell Canada that their products were aging in design and that Northern, with eight thousand employees whose jobs were at stake, would have to design new products of its own and urgently find new places to sell them. "There's nothing, in people or countries or corporations, to compare with the necessity to fight for survival," Marquez asserts. "I don't think you ever really become mature unless you've faced that kind of situation. We did R&D because we bloody well had to. It was do or die."

There was not a single research scientist on the company's staff in 1956; there was no experience in selling in foreign markets and, worst of all, no experience in taking risks. "Risk taking is something which improves with practice" is a Marquez truism. Research is above all risk, and Northern's decision to defend its future via the research laboratory and to define its market as the world established the ethos that would distinguish the Canadian electronics industry during the subsequent three decades.

In 1970, the first black box to become a major commercial triumph for Northern emerged from the research department. It was the SP-1, the first Canadian-made computer-controlled telephone switch. The SP-1 was designed to replace the older, mechanical switches, located in telephone company buildings, which made the physical connections dialled by callers. "The SP-1 wasn't the first electronic switch in the world," says Marquez, "but it was the first damn one that worked." What was most remarkable about the SP-1 was that the computer part of the switch depended on integrated circuits, or silicon microchips, which were designed and manufactured by Northern's own Advanced Devices Centre in the semirural countryside west of Ottawa.

Northern had had some limited experience with semiconductors as early as 1952, when its Montreal engineers began experimenting with the transistors invented by AT&T's Bell Laboratories in 1947. These were essentially miniature switches, capable of changing the direction of an electrical current and having no moving parts or delicate filaments subject to unpredictable failure. The transistor made reliable computers possible. In the next step, first taken in California, several connected transistors were laid out together on one flat piece of silicon, the purest of glass and absolutely impervious to electrical current. The pathways between the transistors were nothing more than impurities carefully laid on the surface of the silicon that would, when ordered to do so by the transistor, conduct a weak flow of current to the next transistor. The silicon sheet thus lost the purity of its insulating quality and became a semiconductor. And the semiconductor's network of miniature transistors acquired the name "integrated circuits," or "microchips."

As is usually the case with new technologies, military strategists were quickest to see the worth of small electrical systems that could control bigger, more brutish machines. The missile race was on, and the less power a rocket needed for its own guidance system, the more punch it could pack in its warhead. Because of early contact with Bell's transistors and its own subsequent commitment to research, Northern was Canada's best hope for keeping abreast. In 1962, the Defence Research Board and the National Research Council asked the company to join them in an intense joint program of research into the powers and potential of the new semiconductors. By 1966, Northern's Advanced Devices Centre was producing 260 different types of semiconductors and, most important of all, had 550 employees learning to run the country's first microchip factory.

The SP-1 electronic switchboard, which used some of those chips, cost Northern $91 million to develop. It quickly became the favourite of the small American telephone companies independent of AT&T. The giant company, for its own needs, remained loyal to its subsidiary, Western Electric. The SP-1 earned Northern sales equal to ten times its development costs before it was surpassed by the company's own subsequent generation of fully computerized switching systems, which emerged in the mid-1970s. Northern's engineers had proven themselves. But as technology advanced, and largely because of Northern's own innovations, the company's management and its owner, Bell Canada, realized that it could no longer finance the massive research and development needed just to remain even with the rest of the world. Northern already had 80 per cent of the Canadian market to itself, but the whole of it would not provide enough revenue to pay for the research activity the company needed to maintain.

Meanwhile, in the United States, the market for telephones and switching equipment had been blown wide open in 1968 by another U.S. antitrust decision against AT&T. The courts ruled that telephone subscribers could connect their own equipment to the lines. The result was that businesses could buy their switchboards and office telephone sets from any company they liked. It was a chance Northern could not ignore, despite the fact that it would mean direct confrontation with its estranged parent, Western Electric.

Marquez hired a team of head-hunters to find his own successor, someone who could lead in the Canadian firm's penetration of Western's home territory. The head-hunters found John Lobb, then fifty-eight years old and a former executive vice-president of International Telephone and Telegraph who had subsequently become president of Crucible Steel Company of Pittsburgh. He was, when Marquez asked him to fly to Montreal for a first meeting in 1970, a partner in a Wall Street firm of investment bankers.

Lobb is a compact, sturdy Minnesotan. His chin is square, his mouth curls down at the corners even when he smiles, and his brow hoods steady, John Wayne eyes. Like his home state's mythical woodsman, Paul Bunyan, Lobb had earned a reputation as a man quick with the axe. Marquez denies that he was recruited to be a hatchet man, but Lobb did know how to fire unproductive people, and Northern had plenty of those. Most important was Lobb's belief that Northern could slice its way into the American market by increasing its sales to the independent telephone companies.

After ninety minutes of talk in his Dorchester Boulevard office, Marquez wanted Lobb for the job, and he called up his own bosses, Bell Canada's president, Robert Scrivener, and the chairman and chief executive officer, Marcel Vincent, to say he was on his way to see them with the man at the head of the short list. Together, Lobb and Marquez walked into Bell Canada's ornate and still imposing old headquarters built in 1929 on a sloping foundation on Beaver Hall Hill. Polished brass handrails set into the building's granite wall still help pedestrians up and down the tilted sidewalk. Marquez remembers that Lobb's principal condition was that he be allowed to introduce a management bonus scheme at Northern to fuel the incentive of the company's executives.

Lobb was more confident of Northern than were its owners, his prospective employers. "Mr. Vincent wanted to know whether I really believed we could successfully invade the American market," he says. "I told them I didn't have any concern about it. It would take a few years and would be hard work, but that was where the business was. More than half of the telephone lines in the whole world were there, and competition by other manufacturers was being encouraged by the American government."

Marquez stepped up to function as Northern's chairman and CEO until 1973, when he reached sixty-five, the company's mandatory retirement age. During his first year as Northern's president Lobb travelled 100,000 miles, imposing his presence on Northern's plants and offices across Canada and forcing managers to account for their performance every month. "There were design engineering problems, there were production problems, very bad marketing problems, and financial controls were weak," recalls Lobb. "Because of the nature of the business and how it had been directed there hadn't been enough strong men attracted to Northern in the last twenty years. So over the next five or six years, we had to replace just about all of the officers." This was traumatic for a company where, Marquez snorts, it was accepted that "you could only get fired for screwing the boss's daughter, and then only if it was on company premises."

Just as Lobb was launching Northern's internal upheaval and simultaneous foray into the U.S. market in 1971, the entire communications industry was radically redirected by an event amid the rich orchard land of the Santa Clara Valley south of San Francisco, where,

25

since 1957, engineers had been at work in small companies dedicated to silicon technology. The work of a young engineer named Ted Hoff was unveiled by his employer, Intel Corporation, at Mountain View. Hoff had managed to shrink an entire computer to fit on a microchip. This, the first microprocessor on a single chip, became a tiny technological virus that would infect every industry, destroying some and forcing others to undergo radical therapy to survive. In none, outside the computer industry itself, did the microprocessor present greater threats, and possibilities, than in the communications industry.

"I came just as there was a real revolution going on in technology," Lobb later reflected. "We were moving from the electromechanical equipment which had been the basis of the Bell System for seventy-five years into complete solid state manufacturing, which means that instead of tool rooms and metal presses and a lot of wiring and assembly we have everything on a large-scale integrated circuit. The chips are inserted into a printed circuit board by machines operated by women. You have women and a lot of engineers running very complex test equipment."

Though Lobb didn't think much of his new company's management, it did have notable engineering strengths in chip design and manufacture. Northern's Advanced Devices Centre near Ottawa had been separated from the company and incorporated in 1969 as Microsystems International, consecrated to the manufacture of microchips. It was, as well, the federal government's chosen instrument for the development of a domestic semiconductor industry. In all, Ottawa sank $37 million in subsidies and loans into Microsystems International.

About the same time Northern had regrouped its research engineers in a new building at the western fringe of Ottawa near the shore of the Ottawa River. This organization, just before Lobb's arrival, became an autonomous subsidiary owned jointly with Bell Canada and called Bell-Northern Research (or simply BNR). It was just a shuttle-bus ride down the road from Microsystems International and nestled like a small college campus amid woodlands, streams, and rolling lawns.

Microsystems acquired chip-manufacturing processes from Intel Corporation and opened a plant in Malaysia. Stock in the new company was offered to the public at ten dollars a share, but Northern retained 88 per cent control. It turned out to be a financial disaster. Prices for microchips were dropping dramatically as production started up, and Microsystems' managers could cope with neither the technology nor the competitive market. Most of them had come from the slow-moving ranks of Northern itself. In 1975, after accumulating losses of $50 million beyond the government's $37 million, Microsystems International was closed down.

This apparent calamity would prove to be the best thing that could have happened to many of Microsystems' 492 laid-off employees. Microsystems had been a nursery of technological and business experience for engineers who would leave to found companies of their own. Two of these were Michael Cowpland and Terence Matthews, who were to become the darlings of Canadian high technology. Their company, Mitel, became the fastest-growing, most glamorous evidence that failure can fertilize success.

Microsystems' building on Moody Drive was handed over to its surviving sibling, Bell-Northern Research, which was just about to divulge to the world Northern's second major black box. Right from its start as an autonomous research company, Bell-Northern's energies had been focused on a project so secret that most of its own staff members were unaware of it. A few senior executives and researchers bound by oath of secrecy mentioned it in whispers as the "E Thing." The E Thing would be more than a super black box. It became the Trojan Horse of the computer age, waiting outside the walls of the telephone system. The E Thing was the first totally computerized telephone switching machine.

A fundamental difference separates the way telephones and computers handle information. Computers deal in simple "digital" pulses of electricity. There are only two types of pulse, one which means *on*, the other which means *off*. The computer interprets the meaning of any particular string of ons and offs according to its program, much the way an observant child might deduce the origin and destination of a freight train by noting the colours and types of its cars. The old telegraph was also a digital system, one which a computer would have little trouble understanding. Each electrical pulse sent down the telegraph line by the operator's clicking key varied from the others only in its duration. The telegraph's Morse code had only two possibilities, long and short. Practised operators interpreted the string of long and short pulses as letters and words in precisely the way computers interpret strings of ons and offs.

The telephone, on the other hand, produces a constant electrical current, which varies in strength according to the sounds generated by a speaker's vocal chords and mouth. The charge travels down the telephone lines in waves of rising and falling intensity. At the receiving end, the waves power an electromagnet which causes a flexible diaphragm to flutter and recreate sound. To a computer, the telephone's wavelike signals are as incomprehensible as, say, the rolling singsong of Chinese to the ear of the average German.

The technology to translate the telephone's analog signals into the digital signals of the computer had existed for years, and many long-distance lines between telephone company central offices already carried calls in digital signals. But the equipment to convert the signals was still too bulky and expensive to be used for local telephone traffic. BNR's engineers produced the first microchip that did the translation job effortlessly and cheaply. Chip technology had progressed so quickly that, in the imagery of a manager of semiconductor production at Northern, if automobile technology had moved as fast as microchip, "a Rolls Royce would now cost two dollars and get 40,000 miles to the gallon."

The E Thing was ready for the world in 1975. Northern Electric and the rest of the world, however, were not quite ready for the E Thing. It represented a giant step away from the familiar electromechanical switches in universal use, and for Northern it meant a radical new role as a world pioneer in the technologies of communications and computers. Many in the company thought it would be nuts to release the E Thing and kill its own successful SP-1, which was earning handsome revenue. But Lobb decided that the E Thing was Northern's opportunity to shed its last ill-fitting hand-me-downs from conservative Bell management, and he decided to transmute Northern into a supranational entity that could measure up to the significance and the business potential of the E Thing.

Lobb first changed the company's staid old name from Northern Electric to the more exciting Northern Telecom. Then he chose, of all places, Disney World for the unveiling in 1976 of the E Thing. Northern Telecom convoked the leading executives of American telephone companies at the Florida playground to declare that "Digital World" had arrived. No longer a secret black box, the E Thing was now christened the SL-1 and headed a complete line of telephone switches and transmission systems that would adopt completely the computer's digital discourse.

When he turned sixty-five, Lobb left Canada to take the presidency of Northern Telecom Incorporated, the U.S. subsidiary he had created, which did not follow its parent's strict rule on retirement. He finally did retire in 1980 in West Palm Beach, Florida, where he lives today. Lobb succeeded in establishing Northern's autonomy from its telephone company parent by inviting the public to share ownership in 1973. Now almost half of Northern's shares are owned by investors. But Lobb's most important parting gift was his public promise that BNR would deliver on Northern's Disney World commitment to produce a full range of digital computers to handle all telephone switching needs. BNR did deliver, and in 1983 the Canadian company calculated that it was still at least two years ahead of its competitors, who were all scrambling to catch up.

At BNR itself, only one of those competitors really seems to inspire worry – the upstart company, just a few minutes drive away, started in 1973 by the two Microsystems International alumni Cowpland and Matthews. "People here even avoid mentioning its name," confided one BNR employee. "They are really paranoid about Mitel." The feeling is perhaps more legitimate fear than groundless paranoia. Much of Mitel's strength comes from a steady infusion of new engineers whose talents, skills, and ideas were developed at BNR. As they drove into the plant grounds on the morning of April 1, 1982, BNR executives were wryly amused to discover flying boldly from the company flag pole a mocking pennant identifying BNR's Moody Drive laboratories and chip plant as the "Mitel Training School."

In many ways BNR does resemble both physically and in its human population an institution of higher learning. More than ninety languages are spoken by the two thousand researchers and support staff recruited to Ottawa from around the world. Including those among the additional thousand employees posted to satellite research centres in Montreal, Toronto, and Edmonton, Bell-Northern has 628 employees with a Master's degree and 180 Doctors of Philosophy. BNR's resemblance to academia is also evident in the prevalence of pompous jargon. One unit calls itself the Design Interpretive Group.

Its vice-president, John Tyson, who wears a clipped professorial beard, sounds eerily like a university sociologist desperate to convince you that what he does is science. Tyson, instead of saying his staff of fifty-five is there to make BNR's designs easy to use, calls it "a functional group representing the behavioural value set" or else a team of "analytical, social cognitive, and environmental psychologists, as well as specialists in software ergonomics" dedicated to "conviviality of interface," which, in English, means easy to use.

The element that distinguishes Bell-Northern from a university is its mandate to produce practical commercial products. Northern's marketing department acts like a thesis adviser to the research engineers, dissuading them from pursuits with doubtful profit potential. But Bell-Northern levies a 10-per-cent tax on all its research contracts with Northern Telecom and puts the money into what it calls a capability fund for research in areas without immediate commercial application. Surprisingly often such projects do become money-makers and set international standards that competitors must match.

Because of the work of BNR, Northern Telecom has become perhaps the most influential telecommunications firm in the world. BNR invented what is now the international standard for the transmission of computer data over telephone lines in "packets," each with its own address, much the way a parcel is posted through the public mails. Canada in 1976 became the first country with a public data network – called Datapac – into which even personal computer owners can dial from their homes. The United States and Europe followed, using the standard developed by BNR engineers. And, significantly, so did IBM, which announced that it would equip its own computers with interfaces to the BNR-designed packet switching system despite its previous attempts to impose its own IBM protocol for the transmission of data in packets.

BNR also designed the first home telephone systems to use optical fibres instead of copper wire. Its Displayphone was the first combination telephone and computer terminal. Most recently, its own home-made software for designing circuit boards has become the IBM standard, purchased by IBM and now leased to IBM clients for an initial fee of $7,800 and $2,600 monthly thereafter.

The most valuable of Northern's contributions to Canada are not technical but human. Without BNR and its lamented sibling, Microsystems International, Canada's family tree of individuals and firms in the microelectronics industry would be a stunted sumac instead of a flourishing pine, perhaps still shallowly rooted but already luxuriantly branched. BNR's files contain a list of twenty-six established firms started by former employees, and the company estimates the full number at closer to one hundred. The Mitel Training School prank erred only in restricting to Mitel BNR's role as supplier of well-trained, ambitious, and confident people to Canada's only industry permeated by the enthusiasm of discovery rather than discouragement and fear.

"I couldn't say it's a role that we deliberately aspire to," says John Elliott, whose twenty-year career with Northern makes him one of the rare research engineers who did not leave the company. "But on the other hand it really does help to have a high-tech infrastructure because there are so many of those places which we call on to help us."

Middle-aged and a bit paunchy, Elliott suggests a tweedy Oxford tutor. Like most engineers, he has preserved a boyish delight in new gadgets, and though his executive duties now keep him away from the laboratory bench, at home he plays with his two personal computers and discusses the latest articles in the popular computer magazines with the same enthusiasm for technical esoterica as a teenaged fanatic.

Elliott retains the English accent he brought to Canada in 1956 when as a young engineer he joined Bell Canada. After returning to London to earn his Ph.D. at Imperial College, he came back in the early 1960s with the flood of British engineers whose own economy could not reward them as much as Canada's. Elliott's specialty was microwave radio systems, which speed telephone calls and computer data between cities, eliminating the need for metal wires. Rising in the company, he took charge of BNR's transmission research, and now as vice-president of corporate development responsible for strategic planning and the stimulation of scientific excellence within a bureaucratic corporation, he has an intimate understanding of what drives his research engineers.

It's not money, it's not working conditions, and it's not, in Elliott's assessment, happiness. "I don't think happy people innovate. It's always the people who want to change the world who are the innovators. They're discontented. Otherwise they don't change

31

things." What does motivate the engineers is the compulsion to see their ideas take material form. "When I drive down the highway and I see a radio antenna sticking up, and I know that if I stop and go in there I'll see the thing that I invented sitting at the bottom of the tower, I find that very satisfying."

Attaining that satisfaction is not simply or solely a matter of technical excellence. Intentionally, BNR's managers foment competitive tension among their researchers, increasing personal stress and squeezing the best efforts from their subordinates. Inevitably, there are losers. Ironically, it's more often from the losers than from the winners of BNR's domestic rivalries that new business successes are born.

"I wouldn't say establishing competing projects is universal or necessarily well planned in advance," Elliott says. "The theory is that you generate as many competing ideas as possible, and you pursue them to the point where one is clearly a winner. Usually within a group there's fairly intense competition for whose ideas will win. But it really isn't quite that straightforward because they borrow one another's ideas all the time as they talk and compete. The purpose is really to get as many people as possible trying to come up with bright ideas and then to put together the right combination of them."

For those whose ideas or projects are rejected, the blow to pride and ambition can make BNR a distinctly unpleasant place to work. "I think it's the chief reason people leave," Elliott muses. "They do not see things moving in the direction they want or as fast as they want. They get frustrated, and they think, 'Gee, I can move things faster if I go elsewhere.'"

Sometimes they plead to come back. "The quickest turnaround I recall is one fellow we promoted to management, and he decided that he really preferred a technical role. He found what seemed to be a very, very attractive position back in his native Holland. So he quit. Sold his house. Crated his furniture and put it on the boat and disappeared. Within a week of his arrival in Holland he decided it was a terrible, terrible mistake, and he was on the transatlantic phone asking to return. He caught a plane and was back here working before his furniture arrived in Holland." That engineer, George DeWitt, is still at BNR, where he works as a senior designer in the microwave radio group, and now accepts the burden of managing the work of others as one of the costs of his own success.

The constant outward flow of well-trained but resentful engineers saves BNR from accumulating layers of unproductive staff. "Sometimes we lose really key people on projects which we are planning to go ahead with but not at quite the speed that they wanted," Elliott says. "But on balance the fact that people do get frustrated, that people do leave, the fact that there are other companies down the road who are now in the same business is good for us. It keeps us on our toes. Competition is always good. We can't afford to sit back."

Curiously, competitive determination to increase Northern Telecom's power in the marketplace can be stronger at BNR than among the parent company's sales forces. The engineers at BNR had to fight to get Northern to commit itself to fully computerized switching systems because that would have meant instant obsolescence of its successful semicomputerized SP-1 system. Elliott recalls, "We really killed SP-1, with a horrible downturn in profitability of our switching business during that transition. A great number of people thought it was very, very silly. But there is no doubt now that Northern totally dominates the switching business in North America."

Protecting that dominance is a challenge when it depends not so much on the excellence of Northern's hardware as on the quality of information in the minds, and in the computers, of BNR. With the merging of computers and communications, the stored information is vulnerable to theft and, worse, sabotage. Because almost every important industrial computer can now be entered via the telephone system by someone sitting at a terminal a mile or a city distant, absolute protection of information is impossible. In 1982, unidentified electronic prowlers managed to work their way, from their computer keyboards, right into the software heart of the Datapac network, which every day flows with sensitive corporate and government information. The damage was light, but it scared the TransCanada Telephone System – the national consortium of telephone companies that handles long-distance and computer communications – which has since tightened up the security of the software.

Elliott considers that the technical specifications of the company's existing products are the least important of its secrets. "Anyone who makes a so-called Japanese copy of an integrated circuit, a camera, or a Displayphone would have done better designing his own. All he's done is copy the past. I think it's a lot more important to protect the strategic plans of the corporation. The business plans are the important part."

It is very difficult to protect totally against infiltration or theft, according to Elliott. "It's a sport. It isn't so much that people want to steal things as that it's fun." The fun, however, can be disastrous to a corporation like BNR. "All you need is someone who's really clever to come in and totally scramble your information data base, and you are in deep trouble," he says. "We have to make sure that information is routinely down-loaded daily onto tape, backed up, and filed away in vaults. At worst, you lose a day's work."

In its crueller meaning, "losing work" is what Northern Telecom and the whole electronics industry are all about. The horrible irony is that every industrialized nation in its drive to increase output per hour of labour and to make as many labour-replacing machines as possible is dedicatedly eliminating the jobs of its citizens. The hope-filled theory that computerization of every aspect of economic activity will create new jobs may eventually prove to be correct, but no one knows better than engineers like John Elliott that the promise of new jobs in manufacturing industries is illusory.

"I suspect," he says, "that any belief that the high-tech business is going to create vast quantities of manufacturing jobs is delusion. It really is going to be a disappointment. There are not going to be large numbers of high-tech manufacturing jobs. I just wish the politicians would understand that. We're going through another revolution like the one in which we threw the vast majority of the population off the farm and into the city. This time we're going to move a very large segment of the population from making things to other forms of employment. I don't think we've come to grips in Canada with the fact that fewer people are going to be working for less time. And certainly not in manufacturing."

It's hard to feel warm and cosy about a multinational corporation with 34,000 employees and forty-eight plants in Canada, the United States, Ireland, Malaysia, and Brazil – especially about one whose essential business is automating other people's jobs out of existence. Northern is one of the ten biggest consumers of microchips in the world, and every chip represents a net loss of jobs for humans. But the difficult truth in this transition from the age of industry to the age of information is that the only variables in the disappearance of existing jobs are *when*, and *whose*. Countries that have the courage to make a bold sacrifice of old industries have the best chances for the biggest share of the new.

In many nations – Great Britain, France, Japan, Germany, and the United States among them – this realization came in the 1970s, and governments bit the bullet. Canada, in that pivotal decade of technological change, was a country distracted by older issues. Control over the national destiny was in the hands of a group of men educated in the classical colleges of Quebec where learning dealt with issues of faith, social theory, and the callings of law, medicine, and the cloth. Business and science were lesser crafts best left to men of more material values. By the time their intellectual squabbles and personality clashes fizzled like damp firecrackers in the early 1980s, the country had wasted another precious generation in one of its periodic exhumations of eighteenth-century European rivalries.

Northern Telecom's current chairman and chief executive officer, Walter Light, an engineer born in Cobalt, Ontario, and a career telephone man, describes Canada as a "technologically underdeveloped nation" which imports more than 80 per cent of its electronics hardware. That represented a trade deficit of $6.1 billion in 1982.

Light is irked by government treatment of companies successful in the new technologies as though they were *nouveaux riches* who ought to be taxed back to humility. In 1980 and 1981, Northern Telecom transferred $90 million to BNR and claimed that the money should be immune from taxation under a federal tax shelter scheme designed to encourage R&D. Northern's diversion of that money offended tax officials who, late in 1982, issued a new set of rules that prevented corporations from sheltering money in such research projects. Light made a personal campaign of getting that tax privilege back, and he largely succeeded when the government reversed itself in 1983. It was hard for someone who, in 1982, earned $541,250 in pay and bonuses to inspire much popular support for corporate tax breaks. But in Light's mind, denying Northern Telecom the right to reinvest that money in research instead of paying it in taxes was a menace to "our survival and the national future."

Equating what's good for a country with what's good for a company made a capitalist bad guy of General Motors' late president Charles Wilson, but in the case of Northern Telecom and Canada, the parallel may be true. Walter Light may be right when he calls telecommunications "as significant a resource to Canada as oil is to Saudi Arabia." And Northern does have some right, after all, to point to itself as the defender of that national resource. While other countries' governments energetically nurtured their academic and industrial strengths in the technologies of microelectronics, in Canada, much of that role of mentor and guardian fell by default to Northern Telecom.

Northern Telecom is now the world's fifth-biggest producer of "custom" microchips, those designed for specific tasks as opposed to multipurpose, off-the-shelf chips, which in industry jargon are called jellybeans. The failure of Microsystems International now well behind it, Northern has mastered the science of chip manufacturing in its Ottawa and San Diego plants, where the chips are made in environments cleaner than a hospital operating room to reduce the threat to the purity of the silicon by pollution from airborne cigarette smoke or cosmetics particles.

More important than the mastery of chip making is the company's triumph over the Canadian business culture of the age of smoke and steel. "The success of companies and countries," according to Light, "has as much or more to do with attitude as it does with assets and abilities. This is nowhere more true than in the global transition from the blue-collar Industrial Age to the white-collar Information Age." And in the Information Age, he warns, Canada's historical strengths of manufacturing and natural resources will be lost increasingly to developing nations.

From Light, the chairman of a company that for most of its life coasted complacently on the assurance of a captive market, now comes adamant disavowal of his country's traditional but self-consuming means of sheltering its industry. "Protectionism can never be a choice for Canada – no matter how seductive and expedient it may appear," he says. "We can defend our own markets and sell our own goods in international markets only if we have better efficiency, higher productivity, and faster innovation than our competitors."

For the second time, Northern has looked south to renew its management strength at the top. Light's successor as president is Edmund Fitzgerald, a fifty-eight-year-old American recruited first to head Northern's U.S. operations, who since May, 1982, has been second to Light in the company hierarchy. Fitzgerald has been quick to adopt the rhetoric of Canada's new class of economic nationalists, concentrated in the industries of the new technologies. In Fitzgerald's assessment, Northern was saved from oblivion by the choice of its leaders in the past decade to transcend the company's ingrown perspective as a manufacturer for the domestic market and become a company based in Canada but international in ambition. "It was clear that Northern Telecom needed to become a leading competitor in international markets. The alternative – to depend only on the Canadian market – would have resulted in languishing performance and probably a slow and inglorious death or digestion by some foreign multinational giant."

Instead, Northern has become a multinational giant on its own and is perfectly at ease inviting the élite of the *Fortune 500* to an exclusive cruise. Northern is the biggest telecommunications manufacturer in Canada and the second-biggest in North America, after its estranged parent, Western Electric. Northern now earns more from its sales in the United States than from those in Canada, and if it were a U.S. rather than a Canadian company, it would hold rank 160 in the 1982 edition of *Fortune*'s exclusive listing of America's top five hundred industrial corporations.

CHAPTER TWO

Going Forth to Multiply

The lane leading to Mitel headquarters at 350 Legget Drive in Kanata, southwest of Ottawa, is a tenuous line between the centuries. Hard against the fence to the left is a working farmer's barnyard, a jumble of haystacks, crooked barns of logs squared with a broadaxe, milling, mooing cattle, and, in the forenoon, a strutting rooster crowing his dominion over the female fowl. On the right, literally crowding into the rooster's territory, sprawls the smoked glass and brown brick world headquarters of Mitel Corporation. Just beyond the low office structure and connected to it by a covered ground level corridor spreads the company's main plant. Behind the two flat buildings, a new six-storey structure will concentrate Mitel's researchers in what President Michael Cowpland describes as a "synergetic cube."

Under the four skylights bubbled over the foyer of the Mitel headquarters, access to the corporate offices is controlled by an attractive young receptionist stationed within a circular counter of chromed and brushed metal. The floor tiles are white, broken by inlaid pathways of blue carpeting. Behind the receptionist's metal doughnut is a matching blue mural of a Mitel microchip, enlarged to four thousand times its true size. The chip was designed for Alberta Government Telephones, and its purpose was to give rural party line customers privacy from the eavesdropping of their neighbours; but it was never installed. From the mezzanine above the microchip mural and down the white walls flows an uninterrupted cascade of greenery. Angled upward from the lobby are two stairways with stainless steel handrails supported by sheets of sheer plexiglass that make voyeurs of innocent visitors sitting on the foam couches against the mirrored wall below.

Michael Cowpland doesn't dispute, even for modesty's sake, that Mitel counts a wildly disproportionate share of beautiful women among its office and managerial staff. "It's a company tradition," he says with a pride he quickly qualifies by asserting that they are not there only for their looks. "We have a lot of women in very powerful positions." Other than that, Cowpland makes no apology for appreciating feminine beauty, and it doesn't take much prodding before he swivels his chair to dig into the drawer of the credenza behind him and produce photographs of three attractive females. The sultry-eyed honey-blonde is his wife, Darlene, and the other two, fresh-faced girls, are his daughters, Paula and Christine.

Most Canadians by now are aware of Michael Cowpland and his ten-year-old company, Mitel. Few, however, realize that Mitel's success has been built on the principle of the better mousetrap. Mitel's business is telephones, but intelligent telephones that can transmit written messages as well as the human voice, connect computers, or lull callers on hold with music. They also make vast amounts of money for Mitel.

The corner location of Cowpland's office, over the entrance to the office complex, is the only obvious perk befitting a company founder and president whose stock fluctuates by literally millions of dollars in value from one week to the next. The office is small, almost over-crowded by a plain desk and a round conference table that would not be out of place in a breakfast nook. De rigueur in the office of any high-tech engineer-entrepreneur, a white marking board hangs waiting on one wall. On another, three photographs of landscapes and a clock with a numberless face list at slightly different angles. Book-shelves are crammed with technical binders, tourist books on Mexico and Czechoslovakia, and *The Blue Book of Canada*. Leaning in a corner is a chrome-plated spade commemorating the sod breaking for Mitel's U.S. national headquarters at Boca Raton, Florida, the younger, burgeoning rival of California's Silicon Valley. On a hook behind the office door waits a blue lab coat which Cowpland throws over his elegant suits for visits to the plants.

Evidence of personal prestige and wealth are actually more visible when the visitor looks out from Cowpland's expansive office win-

40

dow. Just across the paved driveway, a dozen steps from the main entrance, a brick landing pad lies ready for his summons of Mitel's Bell Long Ranger helicopter. Among the few self-indulgent perks that the company's founders have reserved for themselves are the two parking slots closest to Mitel's main entrance, marked "Reserved for Terry" and "Reserved for Mike." Cowpland's spot is filled by a $40,000 metallic-grey Audi Quattra. But the Audi would soon have to make way for its owner's newer toy. Cowpland reports enthusiastically, "Got a Corvette coming in next week. New model. Fantastic car. Corvette has gone from being a relatively unsophisticated sports car to probably better than a Porsche 928. If you read *Road and Track*, the specifications are unbelievable. It exceeds Ferrari's and Porsche's in every dimension." The new Corvette would be the first in Canada. "I love cars. I've got a Corvette now, an older model. And a Jaguar 12-cylinder, last year's model. Super car too. Phantom class Jaguar. Four-door model that really handles well."

Cowpland is a rapid-fire talker, pruning his speech to the cryptic essentials, automatically threshing the English language to glean the grains of meaning and toss away the chaff of unnecessary pronouns and verbs. His accent is unpretentious English middle class with a quasi-Australian twang. He is thin, tightly wound, and hyperactive mentally and physically, his face taut, almost gaunt. His swivel chair moves about his office like an amusement park bumping car as the Mitel president constantly propels himself forward, backward, and sideways for no apparent reason other than to change the view. An appointment with Mike Cowpland is by no means an exclusive right to his time. He carries on several meetings at once, flitting between offices and boardrooms like a superefficient dentist with four patients in separate rooms, all waiting with their jaws open expectantly.

Cowpland was born in 1943 in Bexhill, an English Channel resort town in Sussex. His father, Ronald, was a professional tennis player and ran a restaurant in Bexhill called Sugar and Spice. Both he and Cowpland's mother, Marjorie, were also national-class bridge players who in their later years were hired by cruise ship operators to teach the game to passengers. Cowpland's mother has died, but his father still lives in retirement in Bexhill next to a seaside golf course where he plays between breaks in the rain.

"We were very tight knit. Tennis was the family thing to do

together." Cowpland describes his parents as "medium well-to-do" and says his father's tennis earnings were the source of half the family income. The restaurant and bridge accounted for the rest. "It was an active family. People always zipping in and zipping out."

Michael Cowpland acquired the fanatical family interest in competition. And, of course, in tennis. He started to play when he was seven with his older brother Geoffrey, who is now a vice-president with one of Zimbabwe's major corporations. "We've both kept our tennis up," says Cowpland. "We play regularly every three or four months whenever we happen to be travelling in the same countries." Cowpland competed as a junior for Sussex and then for Imperial College in London where he studied engineering for three years.

His choice of engineering grew naturally from his fascination with motors and mechanics. "I used to rip apart motorbike engines and tune them up. I actually started in mechanical engineering at Imperial College, but after the first year I found it less interesting and I switched into electronic engineering. There seemed to be a lot more room for innovation in it. The state of the art in mechanical engineering is very slow moving these days. Things improve by small percentage points, whereas in electronics things tend to double in capability every two years."

He received his degree in 1964 just as Northern Electric was scouting the university for promising prospects for its plants and laboratories in Canada. Northern offered Cowpland a job and dispatched him to London, Ontario, where he was to work in a production factory. But after just three weeks in London, Cowpland was transferred to the labs of Bell-Northern Research in Ottawa. "That was a pretty important move, though at the time I didn't realize its significance. I was assigned to the designing of electronic telephone equipment, working basically with the actual telephones themselves. That's where I picked up all the telephony knowledge. First exposure."

It was also his first experience of living in a new country, but Cowpland says his migration was a fairly casual affair. "Idea was to go see what it was like. Felt like a one-year shot. It was just an adventure, basically. I didn't feel I was getting cut off or anything. Just a matter of a flight home instead of driving a car." His initial impression of Canada was that it was "a pretty good place." The severity of the climate, however, was not expected. "I bought a used Triumph sports car and was kind of shocked when the starter motor didn't even attempt to rotate on the first really cold day." Cowpland's Triumph was succeeded by an MGB and then an Austin-Healey as one year led to another and the adventure became a permanent migration. Cowpland's secretary at Bell-Northern, Darlene McDonald, was his future wife, and their rapid romantic interest helped keep Cowpland contented in Canada. He quickly moved into tennis circles, too, and would in 1972 win the City of Ottawa championship.

After four years at BNR, in 1968 Cowpland was reassigned to Northern's nearby chip-manufacturing subsidiary, Microsystems International, where, after two years as a chip designer, he was made a manager of circuit design. At the same time, Cowpland was studying part time to earn a Master's degree in electrical engineering from Carleton University. Then, in 1971, he was awarded a scholarship by the National Research Council and began full-time studies for a doctorate. The subject of his thesis was the use of a chip to interpret the musical tones of a touch-tone telephone set and turn them into digital signals that can be understood by computerized switching systems. Upon earning his doctorate, Cowpland returned to Microsystems where his thesis work was converted into a product that Microsystems sold to telephone companies.

The marketing manager at Microsystems was Terry Matthews, another British electrical engineer who had come to Canada from his Welsh homeland to work for Bell Canada. Both men are the same age, and they soon hit it off together. "We got along very well. We had all kinds of ideas. We found that the company was extremely slow moving, so we got frustrated," says Cowpland.

Why Microsystems turned out to be a dud is still a matter for dispute. Northern Telecom's retired chairman Vernon Marquez blames it on the government, saying that Northern went into the chip-making business against its better instincts and only because of Ottawa's pleading and prodding. Cowpland has a simpler explanation: "Terrible management. They put the wrong people in charge. They were going from a monopoly situation, where they were guaranteed a profit, to the world's fastest-moving, most ruthlessly competitive, vicious industry – the chip industry. There's no other industry in the world that's ever doubled its complexity every two years on a compound basis over a period of about sixteen years. So they were coming into this ferocious environment from a very nice, gentlemanly monopoly situation and they got taken to the cleaners very fast."

Cowpland and Matthews fed each other's sense of frustration, convincing themselves that they had ideas that would be sure-fire winners if only management would listen to them. "One was a two-way amplifier system to boost the audio levels in a phone system," recalls Cowpland. "Everything going through the phone system would be louder. I designed it and it worked okay. Another was a speaker in each phone to make it work like a built-in public address system."

Often in the histories of entrepreneurial successes, the original ideas seem, in retrospect, to have been rather flimsy foundations for new companies. They served primarily as justifications for the abandonment of secure but frustrating jobs. "It was more or less a jump into the deep end," remembers Cowpland. "We said, 'Let's do it, because if we don't have a crack at it now we never will.'" Even before actually quitting Microsystems together in 1973, the pair had formed a company they grandly called Advanced Devices Consultants of Canada. Their first venture, however, was hardly appropriate to the name. To get the money they needed to realize their ambitions in electronics, Cowpland and Matthews decided that they would import a nifty cordless electric lawnmower for the Canadian market. "Seemed like a neat gadget," Cowpland says. "The idea was to get some working capital. Didn't work out, though, because the machines weren't suitable for this kind of grass. We brought about three in, but the boat got delayed or something, and they arrived six months late, in the middle of the snow." The three lawnmowers, according to Cowpland, are still sitting unsold in the garage of a friend of Matthews.

Just a week after finally severing themselves from Microsystems, the two new entrepreneurs decided that the name of their company was too cumbersome and dull. "I wanted to get a name that wasn't specific and wasn't too long to say and also that sounded high technology and had some rationale," Cowpland recalls. "That's where Mitel came from. It means 'Mike and Terry electronics.'" Still, history must record that Mitel's first business was lawnmowers, and it failed.

Worse, their schemes for a telephone amplifier and integrated PA system also turned out to be commercial flops. "The customers weren't for real," Cowpland says. "They had said they wanted zillions, but then they kind of fizzled out."

Neither man had previous business experience, and Cowpland credits their first flops with helping to establish Mitel on a sound footing. "It's probably healthier to start off with a failure than a success because you will not get lightheaded. We spent a couple of thousand bucks on the first circuits and the lawnmowers. They were a couple of small failures which forced us to get real very fast."

While catching their second wind, the two pooled what was left of their personal savings. Cowpland made the supreme sacrifice of replacing a Camaro with a two-hundred-dollar Acadian. Matthews sold his car too, and in all they came up with about five thousand dollars. As Cowpland remembers the early days, there was little time for insecurity pangs as they rushed to create a new product before their meagre capital ran out. "I guess we both tend to be very positive thinkers, so we pumped each other up all the time." Mitel rented space in Kanata's Junior Chamber of Commerce building with room for a couple of offices and a laboratory. Darlene Cowpland did the typing. There were five employees in all. The first one was Tom McLeod, who had worked as a chip designer for Cowpland when they were both at Microsystems. McLeod is now Mitel's plant manager of operations.

After their first two products failed in the marketplace, Cowpland went back to the subject of his Carleton University thesis and improved upon it with a better touch-tone decoder than the one he left behind at Microsystems. But Mitel could not afford to have chips made, so Cowpland used standard electronic components soldered together to do the job. The first real sale was to the British telephone maker Plessey Company, and others followed to telephone companies throughout the United States anxious to offer touch-tone service without changing their expensive switching equipment. "Terry would just get on the phone and talk with people he had met when he was in marketing at Microsystems and tell them he had this new part for them."

At last Mitel had a selling product. Then the partners learned that an Oregon company was selling a tone-to-pulse converter that could be installed at the telephone central office itself to handle ten incoming lines. The American company's converter cost $300. Cowpland designed his own with thirty dollars' worth of components to sell for $150. "We got a big chunk of the market right away. Immediately went to about half of the world market. That was our first super success product."

At the same time, the Royal Canadian Mounted Police and the U.S. Federal Bureau of Investigation became customers for what Cowpland describes as "special circuits for surveillance work." He says it was "not necessarily" bugging equipment. "It was kind of useful cash flow work. Not major, but it certainly helped."

Another bit of help arrived thanks to Cowpland's love of parties. "We were invited to a party by our next door neighbour and I met this fellow Kent Plumley and told him all about Mitel. He said that if we ever needed money to let him know. So we called him up and said, 'Yes, we're interested in money.'"

Plumley was a lawyer with the Ottawa firm Gowling and Henderson. He put together an investment group of five lawyers in Ottawa and another five in Toronto, each of whom contributed $10,000. For their $100,000, the investors got 25 per cent of Mitel. But the five in Toronto didn't feel comfortable with their investment. "We were fairly fast moving, and we probably appeared to be out of control to them," says Cowpland. After six months, the Toronto investors sold out to the Ottawa group for $60,000, which meant a safe 20-per-cent profit. "That's got to be one of the worst sell-outs in history," Cowpland gloats. He estimates that the Toronto group's $50,000 investment would now be worth $200 million. The five faithful Ottawa investors are still major Mitel shareholders and the original investor, Kent Plumley, has a seat on the board.

The touch-tone decoders and the undercover cop equipment earned Mitel access to the growth capital that lawnmovers had failed to provide. And the money came just in time, because the company desperately needed more space. In 1975 the local powers finally ordered Cowpland, Matthews, and their growing gang of engineers and technicians to get out of the cramped Junior Chamber of Commerce building. Kanata's mayor, Marianne Wilkinson, is sympathetic to the needs of the entrepreneurs who have made her city the focus of the country's economic hopes, but things had gone too far. "Pretty soon they had twenty-five employees, and they were parking all over the streets. The building wasn't zoned for business. We kicked them out for breaking the by-law." Mitel moved to a warehouse in Kanata's industrial park but then overflowed that into seventy trailers like those used for bunking in frontier construction camps. "We had to close our eyes to the holding tank they used as a sewage system for two hundred employees," she says. But there were no hard feelings, and in January 1979 Mayor Wilkinson was invited to a sod-turning ceremony – in a blizzard – to mark the start of construction of Mitel's new headquarters and plant. These buildings didn't manage to contain the expansion in Kanata, but they at least provided the company with a physical focus and its first fixed address.

Mitel had in 1976 purchased the plant of a bankrupt chip maker in Bromont, Quebec, an exclusive community catering to equestrians and high tech in the Eastern Townships southeast of Montreal. Since then, Mitel has made the microchips for its own products and for outside customers. In the process, it has become an innovative leader in chip manufacturing and has even sold its manufacturing methods to competing telephone makers. The Mitel complex has grown by construction and acquisition not just in Kanata and Bromont but in Ogdensburg, N.Y., Boca Raton, Puerto Rico, Mexico, Ireland, Wales, Germany, New Zealand, Hong Kong, and Japan. Mitel is now taking the advantages of advanced technology jobs to Buctouche, N.B., and Renfrew, Ontario, areas of desperate dependence on disappearing industries.

Mitel's migrations through the industrial parks of the world were impelled by Matthews's brilliant selling of the ever-more-sophisticated telephone systems Cowpland's engineers designed back home in Kanata. Events were well timed for Mitel. Court decisions in the United States opened up the market for business telephone systems by ordering the telephone companies to allow customers to plug their own equipment into the networks. At the same time in Canada, the federal government was ready to throw money at companies willing to jump into the microelectronics industry. Mitel, along with Northern Telecom, made the most of those opportunities.

As Mitel gained momentum in the mid-1970s, Cowpland decided to apply the newest chip technologies to an old product, the private branch exchange or PBX. The PBX is the telephone exchange in a private business which connects the trunk lines from the outside world to the network of extensions within the business itself. Cowpland set out to make one having a microprocessor to control its operations, though the actual routing of calls was still done by little mechanical switches. It was, on a small scale, similar to what Northern Telecom was doing with the big switching systems designed for use by the telephone companies themselves.

With grants from the National Research Council, Mitel built its chip-based PBX, and it worked. But Cowpland was dissatisfied with the size and bulk of the whole apparatus which included transformers for each telephone line. All the older PBXs had similar transformers and Mitel's didn't really look any different, even though internally it was a leap ahead. As Cowpland tells the story, "Looking at it, it became obvious to me that the secret was to get rid of the transformers, and that's when I designed the solid face interface. That enabled us to shrink our size because otherwise we'd have ended up with a me-too PBX. Once we came up with our box, people couldn't believe how small it was, and of course, the power requirement was way down. That's why we have now become the world's number one PBX vendor. When you offer a better product at a lower price you can make a very rapid penetration." The box, the Mitel SX-200, was first sold in 1978 and is still the company's main product.

Since the SX-200, the company has added a series of smaller phone systems right down to the Talkto, designed for homes. This labour-saver can answer the door, monitor alarms and – reviving one of the partners' original schemes – perform as an intercom and paging system to track down the kids.

Now Mitel is attacking the other end of the market, the big companies with hundreds of trunk lines and thousands of extensions and a lot of computers competing for lines to exchange information. Mitel's SX-2000 is literally a black box, the size of a refrigerator. The first fully digital PBX, it can handle up to ten thousand telephones.

The SX-2000 brings Mitel into direct, head-bashing competition with Northern Telecom. Mitel's machine is smaller than Northern's equivalent SL-1, uses less power, and transmits data between computers twenty-five times faster. Each company wants its own machine to become the hub of the so-called electronic office. Both Mitel and Northern are courting the computer makers to make their machines compatible with their telephone switching systems. Mitel seemed to have an enormous advantage over Northern until June 1983, when it lost an agreement with IBM to marry the SX-2000 to IBM computers. IBM would also have marketed Mitel's machine. It was because the Kanata company couldn't get the bugs out of the SX-2000's software as quickly as promised that IBM broke the engagement and took up with Rolm instead.

There were other disappointments too. Mitel sales in 1982 totalled $204,129,000, just 7 per cent of Northern Telecom's but a 25-percent rise over its own revenues of the previous year. This would be justification for wild rejoicing at most companies. At Mitel, however, there was moderate funk among people used to doubling sales from year to year. Cowpland handed over responsibility for day-to-day management of Mitel to Executive Vice-President Donald Gibbs, planning to don his blue lab coat more often as he returned his attention to product development. Then, for the first three months of 1983, the firm posted its first loss ever as a publicly traded company as the general economic recession caught up with it. A new plant in Burlington, Vermont, was closed to save money, and construction of a plant in France was postponed. Development of Mitel's Skyswitch satellite telephone system was also cancelled.

The bad news obscured some good tidings, including the start-up of EMX Telecom of Maryland, a joint venture between Mitel and American Satellite Company, which will supply communications services using the SX-2000 as the link between telephone lines and space satellites. Mitel succeeded in getting approval to sell small business telephone systems in Japan and concluded a three-million-dollar distribution agreement with that country's Pioneer Electronics Corporation. While sales dropped slightly in Canada, those in the United States – where twenty-three Bell telephone companies use Mitel equipment – increased in 1982 to 52 per cent of the company's total revenues while sales in Europe and other countries increased even more rapidly to 31 per cent of the total. There was also partial consolation for the falling out with IBM in agreements to mate the SX-2000 with computers made by Digital Equipment Corporation and International Computers of England.

To some investors, the bloom had faded from the Mitel rose and the company lost its glamour on the stock market. But the setbacks of

1983 probably are more significant as indicators that Mitel has reached maturity as a major player. It can now afford, after all, to lose more than $4 million in three months without threat to its existence, and it continues to invest in its own future by spending increasing amounts on research and development.

Mitel now employs more than five thousand people around the world, of whom eighteen hundred communicate with each other not by telephone but by electronic mail, sending written messages between their computers. Though Cowpland loves the machines, he is most proud of Mitel's informal ambience. "People around here are used to the fact that we're really down to earth. Everything's first names. Nobody's better than anybody else. Which is important, because you want to make sure they don't feel intimidated. If the ideas don't flow, then the whole thing grinds to a halt. Especially in high tech, the people who know the most tend to be at the lower levels with the hands-on jobs. So if you don't get that communication flowing you end up with an ivory tower approach where all the big honchos think they know everything and make the decisions. Then you get into trouble."

Cowpland's car mania overflows into employee incentive programs. Mitel manager Ernest Childs was awarded a DeLorean sports car for winning a competition to recruit new workers to Mitel. Cowpland takes pride, too, in the success of Mitel's women workers who have made careers beyond the bounds normally dictated by their education and experience. "We started off the company saying, 'We don't care what your paper qualifications are as long as you can do the job.' And that applied to women as well as men. Penny Bunge is one of the cases we point to. She came in as an $8,000-a-year filing clerk and she is now running our corporate purchasing. Massively responsible job. And that's in only four or five years. We'll give people rapid progress, provided they can do a hell of a job."

Mitel first offered stock to the public in 1979 and encourages employees to become owners through a profit-sharing plan that lets them spend up to 20 per cent of their salaries on company stock priced below market value. Mitel's biggest single shareholder remains Matthews, with 7.3 million, or 18 per cent, of the company's 38 million outstanding shares. Cowpland holds 6.5 million. Cowpland's personal wealth can change, as it did during the recession of 1982 when

Mitel stock dipped from $38 to $16.75, by $138 million in a year without really affecting his life. He says lightly, "It fluctuates wildly up and down on paper. In terms of cash, I'm a borrower."

Ten years after founding Mitel, Cowpland was still living on the same Ottawa street where he was when he quit Microsystems ("We find it's quite adequate"). But he was awaiting completion of a new Ottawa townhouse and also owns a condominium in Fort Lauderdale. Real luxury is reserved for a million-dollar estate that developer Robert Campeau originally built as his residence on the Ottawa River near Dunrobin. Cowpland renovated the place, adding a disco with the Mitel logo embedded in the dance floor, a solarium, a slide from the rooftop to the pool, and courts for tennis, racquetball, and squash. Cowpland calls the property Stoke Lacey after the English home town of his grandfather. The country place, he says, "is largely for business entertainment, plus it's fun for the family occasionally." Cowpland threw an impromptu Christmas get-together there in 1982, dispatching a helicopter to pick up Prime Minister Trudeau and bring him out for the party.

Terence Matthews has been more sedentary in his home life, preferring to remain in the same modest house in Kanata that he owned before Mitel began. Only a decade later did he decide a bigger place would better serve his growing family, but he didn't want to leave the neighbourhood. Unfortunately, there was just nothing bigger nearby. So in 1982, Matthews called his friend the mayor. "He was ready for a bigger house, and he was concerned about security as well," confides Wilkinson. "So he called me and asked where he could get land within walking distance of where he was. We had a ten-acre site which was zoned for apartments. We rezoned it for seven homes. There will be six homes and a gatehouse, fenced in. The homes will be for Matthews and some senior Mitel executives and will cost in the range of half a million dollars. We already call it The Compound," she says.

Matthews prizes his privacy to a degree uncommon among the younger leaders in the microelectronics industry. "I have a very nice little family, and I don't like having to defend my privacy all the time. I want to lead a normal life, with my telephone number listed in the book." Instead, he complains, "I get called up by all kinds of kooky brains." Stubborn as only a Welshman knows how to be, he adamantly refuses to recount his life and thoughts for the public record. "I'm not trying to be awkward. I just don't want my name thrown around all the time."

Matthews's refusal to open up is both a pity and a loss because through the bluster filters a warmth and sympathy that may have as much to do with Mitel's success as his constant jetting about the world selling its products. It is because of the ambience and the policies of companies like Mitel that capitalism and business at present are enjoying unaccustomed favour with a citizenry soured on politicians as protectors and providers of economic well-being. There may well be a more generous sensitivity to the human condition in entrepreneurs such as Matthews, who decided to locate Mitel's main British factory in his native South Wales, a land ravaged by the first industrial revolution and now left bleeding with abandoned coal pits, exhausted steel mills, and a population in need of renewed pride and economic hope.

In contrast to his partner's horror of public attention, recognition holds no terrors for Mike Cowpland. He maintains a visible social life centred on his two tennis clubs in west end Ottawa and the Queensview Racquet and Nautilus Club, which he also owns. The Queensview club, located at the hub of high-tech activity in Kanata and suburban Ottawa, has become the noontime rendezvous for successful electronics entrepreneurs. The club has an excellent restaurant that serves fresh-cut french fries rather than frozen facsimiles despite Cowpland's business associations with New Brunswick food magnate Harrison McCain. There are also salads for members who want to cultivate the lean and mean look. The club's female staff seems to be drawn from the Mitel mould of extravagant attractiveness, while the nearby thumping of squash and racquetballs sets a beat conducive to fast-paced business deals.

Cowpland counts Montreal architect David Simmonds, who rebuilt the Dunrobin estate, among his personal friends. His circle of friends also includes stockbroker Ron Potts, Ottawa Rough Rider Tony Gabriel, restaurateur Frank Lambros, and builders William Teron, Bob McElligott, and Robert Nihon. Ottawa helicopter company operator Ross Tuddenham has become a friend and business confidant after meeting Cowpland on the tennis court. Though squash and raquetball are part of Cowpland's regular sports regimen, tennis is still the focus of his private and much of his business life. He abhors airy thinking and mystification of simple things and refuses to attribute any particular role to his competitive tennis playing in his business success. "It's just a source of enjoyment." Tennis partners include Canadian Davis Cup player and coach Dale Power. "I don't like just sort of rallying," says Cowpland. "If I'm better than somebody else I'll give him a handicap, but when I play Dale he'll give me about fourteen points, which means that on a good day I can beat him, and at least I know he's trying."

Cowpland plays tennis most frequently with lawyer Glen St. John, who was the manager of his personal financial affairs even before Cowpland drew him into his tennis and business circle. St. John was born in Regina in 1941 but raised in Ottawa, where he studied political science and was, from 1960 to 1963, the handsome quarterback of the Carleton University Ravens. Then, when he was a law student in Montreal, he played quarterback for the McGill Redmen and, for the 1963 season, he played quarterback professionally for the Montreal Alouettes.

After working as a small-town lawyer in Minnedosa, Manitoba, and as a litigation counsel with the federal government, St. John earned a Master of Business Administration degree from Carleton and established his own financial and tax-planning firm in the late 1970s. Seeking a replacement for football as an outlet for his athletic and competitive energies, he took up tennis. "I found it a difficult game to come to later in life," he recalls. "Mike and I struck up a competitive relationship on the court, though he won all the time. We continued to play and discussed different matters along the way, and my tennis improved while his went down marginally because of his tremendous involvement in Mitel. Today, we're pretty well matched." Even as business partners, their relationship remains centred on the tennis court. "We just go out and play like crazy fools, shake hands at the end of it, and get down to business. I think that latent competitiveness was something we respected in each other. We each carry that forward into our business relationships, and we've often said that business is really a game just like tennis. What counts is whoever has the most points at the end of the game."

Cowpland's affairs, when St. John took over their management in 1980, included a portfolio of investments in small technology companies in Ottawa held by a personal investment firm called Krystalla Corporation, an amalgam of his daughters' names. St. John then began on his own to invest in Ottawa high tech, and by 1981 the two decided it would be wise to fold Cowpland's $150,000 investment portfolio and St. John's $40,000 in investments into a new venture capital company. They called it Bytec – a triple pun evoking Ottawa's original name, Bytown, the computer term *byte* and the expression *high tech*. St. John became Bytec Management Corporation's president. Cowpland makes the important investment decisions but without sacrificing the attention he gives to Mitel. St. John says, "You have to realize that Mike's a different kind of person. He has a great mind and an ability to continually absorb facts and challenges."

Bytec is a reflection of its founders' personalities and perspectives. St. John set up shop not in a plush downtown suite but in a corner office off the lobby of the Queensview Racquet Club, as though to imbue Bytec with an approach to business as a healthy, competitive game. Although most of its investments are in the Ottawa area, some are in California and others in Florida. Like most Canadian high-tech entrepreneurs, St. John has matured beyond Canada's traditional insecurities and looks to the United States not as a threat but as an opportunity. "It's nice to be competitive with the Americans, who are the best in the world at most everything. I probably could have been a damn good American," he says. "I respect the American businessman. There's no reason the Canadian businessman can't be as good if not better."

Bytec's list of investors grows as more and more people want to rub against the Cowpland magic. Low-tech capitalists Conrad and Montegu Black covered their bets on failing smokestack industries by buying into Bytec and Harrison McCain did the same. Bytec investments include shares in a dozen firms and products as diverse as Imaginamics Incorporated, which makes electronic desk blotters with built-in telephones and calculators, NABU Manufacturing Corporation, which has invented a system of home computers that connect to a central program bank by cable television, and Systemhouse Limited, a major computer program maker that Bytec saved from death. In some cases, Bytec's bets were duds. One of Cowpland's first investments, Kombi Office Automation Systems, which made furniture, failed in 1982. Simultaneously, a California company called Magnusson Computers Incorporated in which Bytec held an interest just had time to sue its former owner for making off with company secrets before going bankrupt.

Other Bytec investments have been more fruitful. One wintry evening in November 1981 Cowpland and St. John boarded a chrtered executive jet in Ottawa and flew to Montreal to have a look at a quickly growing company called Comterm. The company had once been a part of another Montreal firm called Central Dynamics, but when that company became paralysed by a lack of cash to develop new products in 1978, its vice-president of finance, Laurent Nadeau, and a group of engineers bought their way to independence, setting up Comterm as a corporation on its own.

Comterm proceeded to corner the Middle Eastern market for bilingual computer terminals capable of displaying Arabic or Roman characters. From a technological perspective alone this was, in the parlance of software engineers, a non-trivial task since Arabic characters are not only displayed from left to right but can change their shape depending on their location within a word. The Arabian market was also fraught with political hazard. Comterm's fate was nearly sealed in 1978 when it borrowed heavily to produce Persian computer terminals for Iran, only to lose the order in the mess of the revolution that overthrew the late Shah. The company was saved by an order for two thousand Loto Québec gambling terminals, after which it returned to the Middle Eastern market and supplied hundreds of Arabic terminals and printers to Saudi Arabian government offices.

Laurent Nadeau is a soft-spoken, cultured accountant who was born in 1934 to a farming family near Thetford Mines. Nadeau chose a path unusual for French-speaking Quebeckers when, in the 1950s, he studied commerce at McGill University. He had enrolled as a night student before speaking a word of English. He was suspicious of the fast-talking Cowpland and his colleague, St. John, when they first called on Comterm's plant in suburban Pointe Claire. Worried that perhaps the Mitel president wanted to spy on Comterm's engineering projects for the benefit of Mitel's own research activities, Nadeau scheduled the plant tour for the end of the working day when his engineers would be on their way home and their work safely locked out of sight. "I didn't want to reveal any secrets without knowing the purpose of their visit," he recalls.

But the three soon developed trust in each other, and after visiting Comterm's facilities in the suburb of Pointe Claire, they went off to a modest local restaurant where over supper they agreed to a $750,000 investment by Bytec in Nadeau's firm. In return, there would be seats on the Comterm board for Cowpland and St. John, who grew to respect Nadeau's cautious business sense.

Bytec's biggest single investment was the purchase of the Ottawa computer maker Dynalogic Corporation, which, with Bytec money and encouragement, designed the Hyperion personal computer and proceeded to manufacture it in a new factory on the southern outskirts of Ottawa. His own Hyperion has become Cowpland's newest hobby in a way that recalls his love of cars. "It's a dynamite machine. Nicest-looking personal computer in the world, and it's very high performance, too." The first production Hyperion left the factory in January 1983. In the ensuing months it would become not just another plaything for Cowpland but the focus of a plan to repeat the Mitel story – this time not with telephone equipment but with computers for businesses, schools, and homes.

CHAPTER THREE

The Key to the Kingdom

Graeme Scott has been a full-time employee of Bell-Northern Research since 1967. Each morning when Scott leaves for work, he steps out of the kitchen of his home on Kingsford Crescent in the centre of Kanata, turns before reaching the front door and, in stocking feet, mounts the stairs to a bedroom converted into an office and atelier. Looking like a sea captain on the bridge, with his white beard and moustache, Scott settles into a swivel chair and flips switches to send power surging through the circuitry of the machines that envelop him. At his left is a Northern Telecom Display-phone that serves as his electronic mailbox for the passage of written messages between his home and BNR headquarters just across the agricultural Green Belt that separates Ottawa and its immediate suburbs from Kanata. On his right are an IBM Personal Computer and an Apple II. Scott seems to live the life of a teenaged "hacker" who grows pallid from too many late nights squinting into the screen of his Apple while obsessively improving his latest program.

The difference is that Scott, at fifty-one, is one of BNR's highly paid electronics geniuses and carries the impressive official title of Manager of Intelligent Terminal Applications. As a consequence of his own work making communications terminals increasingly sophisticated, Scott realized three years ago that there was no real need for him to suffer the inconvenience of having an office at BNR itself. So he dispensed with it and moved his work home to the bedroom vacated by a grown-up daughter. His link with BNR is the telephone line connected to his three computers, and undisturbed by social trifles and office politics he has peace to create his magical programs, which make computers communicate with more order and elegance than most humans are capable of. "It's great," Scott says of his working situation. "No administrative bullshit."

Scott also runs, from this bedroom office, his own company called Arrow Micro Software, which provides a commercial outlet for some of his experimental work that is of no direct use to BNR. Scott's communications programs for the Apple II and IBM Personal Computer are beyond doubt the most sophisticated available anywhere. They can actually transmit themselves down telephone lines to another personal computer and then allow users at each end to work simultaneously on the same document. One user could, for example, change a word on the screen of his Apple in Vancouver, and the change would appear at the same instant on the screen of another Apple in Halifax. Scott's software also employs techniques of data compression and multiplexing and can transmit text and pictures much faster than normally possible over the telephone line. Users can carry on a written conversation across the lower edges of their screens while they watch the progress of the transfer of a document or graphic image in the space above. The manifold performance of Scott's programs is unique in the world and surpasses anything else commercially available.

Scott did have early experience in operating a business from a bedroom. When he was eleven and living as a student at Edinburgh's Fettes College, Scott built twenty-six radios from scratch and sold them to fellow boarders. But it is more because of the social and working culture that has evolved in the community of Kanata that Scott can live the reality of the electronic cottage predicted in futurist writings.

Kanata itself was an exercise in futurism. It began in the 1960s as a vision of perfection in the mind of Ottawa developer William Teron. The builder, who was later appointed president of the Central Mortgage and Housing Corporation and now carries on an international construction business that builds plants in Canada and overseas for Mitel, wanted to create a totally planned and self-sufficient community. He chose a 3,200-acre tract of March Township, ten miles west of Ottawa near the south shore of the Ottawa River, to realize his dream town.

March Township's early economic history is in many ways a miniature of Canada's own. First, in the early 1780s, after the land had been ceded to the Crown by the Mississauga Indians, the area's forests were stripped of stately white pine to make masts for the British fleet. Then followed several decades of settlement by refugees from famine and economic oppression in the British Isles who tamed the land ravaged by the loggers. Another sizeable group consisted of pensioned British soldiers who remained in Canada after the War of 1812. Most of March Township's settlers were poor and erected simple log shanties on land that wasn't much richer. The industrial revolution reached the area in 1833 when steamboats began regular service between nearby Fitzroy Harbour and Aylmer on the Quebec side of the Ottawa River. But when in 1888 the Ottawa, Arnprior and Renfrew railway arrived in March Township, river travel declined. Meanwhile the logging industry came to a stop, and manufactured goods brought by rail destroyed the market for local artisans. Finally, because of its marshy terrain and clay soil, March Township never did prosper as a farming region.

The land's low agricultural value meant that Teron could assemble the tract for his community cheaply. He called it Kanata, an Indian word meaning "village" that Jacques Cartier had mistakenly understood to be the name of the country itself. Teron built a tree-studded community of winding roads, footpaths, and rustic homes, but it remained, in its early years, just another bedroom suburb of Ottawa. Kanata had everything for its residents but jobs.

In 1970, Teron sold his development company and with it control over Kanata's destiny. The buyer was Campeau Corporation, Robert Campeau's real estate and construction company, and Kanata residents worried about losing their sylvan calm to high density housing. Defence of the concept of Kanata as a planned community was taken up by a local monthly newsletter, the *Kanata Standard*, whose political reporter was a young mother with a university education in urban geography. Marianne Wilkinson had moved to Kanata in 1968 because its planned development appealed to her academic commitment to urban order.

The uncertain future of the community inspired Wilkinson to run for a seat on the March Township Council, the closest thing Kanata had to local government. She won and persuaded the council to adopt a planning policy for the first time, a formidable administrative responsibility for a municipality with just four office workers and a road crew. Wilkinson mobilized the residents themselves into planning committees, a move that not only solved the staff problem but also established a tradition of local government that still blurs the line between elected officers and volunteers. Kanata invented the "cluster leader," described as the "interface" between the residents of a small group of homes and the municipal administration.

The sudden political mobilization ensured Campeau's respect for the community's spirit, and the developer and elected representatives have coexisted harmoniously since then. Kanata became a separate municipality in 1978. Marianne Wilkinson was elected its first mayor and has been re-elected twice. Kanata is now a boom town of twenty thousand residents and has forty industries, all of them related in one way or another to advanced technologies, from lasers to satellites. Wilkinson uses the fashionable term "synergy" to explain Kanata's sudden growth from pastoral subdivision to mecca for microelectronic industry. Synergy is a combination of things and events whose total effect is greater than what would be expected if each one made its impact independently. In high-tech industry, synergy means that companies working in close proximity to each other are stronger than they would be working in isolation, and their proximity creates a gravitational pull upon yet other enterprises and potential entrepreneurs. So intense is the synergistic attraction even within Kanata, says the mayor, that the Kanata North Business Park, around Mitel, is jammed, while the Kanata South Business Park, just two miles away, is empty. "New companies particularly," she says, "have to be where the synergism is."

Unlike the old industries that were almost expected to blight their surroundings, high tech demands that its environment be pleasant for people. "It is imperative to maintain the quality of life," Wilkinson says. "That's why the high-tech people come here and that's why they stay."

Wilkinson's indulgence toward the fast-moving entrepreneurs is another reason why her town is a haven for high tech. "Where else would a businessman call to get permission to put in a helicopter pad right away on land he didn't even own yet?" she asks. Similarly, half the planned houses in a new subdivision called Bridlewood were sold even before the zoning laws had been changed. The mayor makes no apologies for her alliance with the industrial interests. "I fell in love with the small business ideal, and I have a feel for high tech," she says. "You have to be a little nuts. But you have to have vision, a feel for what will be."

The spark that set off Kanata's synergistic growth as Canada's most concentrated cluster of advanced technology enterprises is often identified as the decision by Digital Equipment of Canada to build its new plant there in 1972. In reality, the first advanced technology plant in Kanata was the commercial products division of Atomic Energy of Canada opened in 1965. In contrast to the Crown corporation's better-known nuclear power technology, which is literally a throw-back to the steam age with its use of polluting and wasteful nuclear reaction to boil water and turn the turbines of electricity generators, its Kanata division produces radiation machines for cancer therapy and industrial tasks. At the same time, in the mid-1960s, there were just beyond the boundaries of Kanata Northern Electric's research laboratories, later to become BNR, and its neighbour the federal government's Communications Research Centre. Microsystems International also spent its brief life in the same neighbourhood.

Many employees of these research and manufacturing establishments chose to live in Kanata. This fact is the critical one in explaining Kanata's surge as the focal point of the new technologies in Canada. Mitel is in Kanata because that's where Terence Matthews lived when he and Michael Cowpland quit Microsystems. The equally important choice of Kanata a year earlier by the Canadian subsidiary of Digital Equipment Corporation was also abetted by the fact that its president, Denzil Doyle, had been one of the first dozen residents in the town when he settled with his family in 1965.

But only a superficial understanding of boom town Kanata is possible without going back to the Second World War, when the foundation was laid for Ottawa's role as research centre for the nation. Just as Kanata's little start-up companies thrive on its synergistic climate, Kanata itself could not have become Silicon Valley North without being in the environs of Ottawa, which had strong traditions in industrial and governmental research when Kanata was still cow pasture.

Wartime work by the National Research Council focused on electronic military equipment, and in 1948 the demand for such electronics created the region's first important high-tech company, Computing Devices of Canada, which was and remains located in Bells Corners, not far from Kanata. The federal government's presence as an extravagant consumer of advanced technology and the sympathy of government purchasers for young Canadian-owned firms have ever since been critical factors in the Ottawa area's high-tech success story. At the same time, inventions by government agencies, such as the National Research Council's Crash Position Indicator for downed aircraft or the Communications Research Centre's Telidon, have been turned over to private enterprise for development as commercial products.

Ottawa's involvement in the critical area of space and communications satellites has had obvious benefits but is also severely crippling Canadian growth in space technology because of persistent belief in cultural protectionism within bodies such as the Canadian Radio-television and Telecommunications Commission. The federal government's technological contribution to space communications is immense, but its attempt to manipulate the technology for political and cultural ends is a disaster and threatens to cost the country its leadership in satellite communications.

In 1962, Canada's Alouette I satellite was launched into space atop an American rocket. Seven years later, a federal law created a unique private company owned jointly by the government, the telephone companies, and CNCP Telecommunications. Telesat Canada's mission was to guard Canada's place at the forefront of space communications and it rushed to get its first commercial satellite into space. Mary Czapala, a supermarket worker in the Italian-speaking Montreal suburb of St. Leonard, won a contest to name the satellite. Marshall McLuhan was one of the judges who selected her suggestion, "Anik" – the Inuit word for brother.

A more controversial choice was that of a contractor to build the satellite itself. Both contenders, RCA and Hughes Aircraft, were American owned. RCA appeared to be the more reliable and less expensive choice, but Telesat Canada president David Golden awarded a $31-million contract to Hughes because of the California firm's commitment to subcontract 20 per cent of the work to Canadian companies. Thus, parts of the three Anik A satellites were made by Northern Electric in Lucerne, Quebec, and by Spar Aerospace Products of Malton, Ontario. Meanwhile, teams of surveyors and construction workers fanned out across the country, building the network of earth stations that would send and receive satellite microwave signals carrying television broadcasts, telephone conversations, Telex messages, and flows of data between computers. On November 9, 1972, Anik A-1 departed Cape Canaveral aboard a U.S. Delta rocket, emblazoned with the red-and-white Maple Leaf, for a spot in the southern sky where it settled into an orbit exactly matching the speed of the earth's rotation, thus providing a motionless target for the earth stations spanning Canada below. A second Anik A sent into space in 1973 provided Alaska with television signals from the lower forty-eight states until 1975, when the United States launched its first domestic communications satellite, more than two years behind Canada's.

The CRTC dealt the first blow in what seems to be an obsessive, continuing campaign against Telesat in 1977 when it used its regulatory powers to disallow the company's association with the telephone companies as set out by Parliament. The federal cabinet reversed that ruling several months later, but it forced Telesat to a virtual halt in the interval. Telesat had to suspend its choice of a builder of its third series of satellites, called Anik C. Hughes eventually won the order, but this time Canadian content was up to 40 per cent. Then, in 1979, the prime contract for the newest Telesat satellites, the Anik D series, went to the Canadian firm Spar Aerospace, whose satellite division is located in Ste-Anne-de-Bellevue, Quebec. Anik D-1 was launched by rocket from Florida in August 1982, and in November Anik C-3 – along with the similar-appearing American satellite partly owned by IBM – was delivered gently to its orbit by the space shuttle whose long, jointed arm was made by Spar.

Whether Telesat's Anik satellites can compete commercially with the increasing number of privately owned American competitors depends on its bureaucratic nemesis, Ottawa. The CRTC has ruled against Telesat requests so often that Telesat's current president, Eldon Thompson, has undertaken an open verbal war with the regulatory agency, saying that the risk of retaliation is irrelevant because relations now are so poor that Telesat has nothing to lose.

63

Thompson has compared CRTC constraint of Telesat's freedom to set rates and choose its customers to Canada's self-inflicted technological wounding when it cancelled the Arrow jet fighter project in 1959.

Canadian protectionism, cultural and economic, has been a sometimes fatal burden upon Canadian high-technology ventures. One of Canada's few high-tech leaders with long enough experience to have an established perspective on the industry's evolution is William Hutchison. Though just forty-five, he is already an old-timer in an industry where a year is an eon. Hutchison was a key figure in the establishment of a Canadian-owned computer industry and he continues his leadership role both as a director and interim president of the Telidon firm Infomart and as president of his own Toronto consulting firm.

Hutchison is a Canadian economic patriot, a founder and now chairman of the Canadian Advanced Technology Association which lobbies in Ottawa for the kind of tax and trade treatment that will allow high-tech industry to flourish. Older generations of economic nationalists hid behind the skirts of protectionism. Hutchison, like all the country's ambitious high-tech businessmen, is convinced that total free trade with the United States is essential to Canada's future as a continuing economic entity. Though tariffs are being gradually eliminated under the international General Agreement on Tariffs and Trade, there remains a federal sales tax of 10 per cent on imported goods that has a destructive effect on Canada's ability to import the machines and components necessary for high-tech manufacturing, research, and software development. Hutchison knows at first hand the stifling effects of Canadian protectionism. Barriers of tariffs and taxes succeeded only in prolonging the agony of Canada's shoemakers and copy-cat manufacturers who did little research on their own, and they killed the first serious attempts to build computers in Canada.

Hutchison was born in northern Ontario and grew up in Hamilton and Glasgow, Scotland, as his engineer father moved between jobs in mines and factories. Hutchison followed in his father's footsteps by enrolling in engineering at McGill University. He was not a dedicated scholar and behaved more like an artsman than an engineer. He was, during his years at McGill, president of the Students' Union, president of the football band, president of Sigma Chi, president and drummer of the McGill Symphonic Band, editor-in-chief of the

McGill yearbook, and a member of the original 1957 cast of McGill's satirical review *My Fur Lady*. "Academically, I was near the bottom of the class," he recalls. "I was never a good engineer in the oscilloscope and laboratory sense."

Summers, Hutchison worked as an installer's helper for Ontario Northland Communications and then, before graduating from McGill, he went to work for Bell Canada in Montreal designing mobile radio systems and data communications circuits. "That's where I got my first exposure to computers and realized that that was where the growth would be," he remembers. In 1962, Hutchison moved to Toronto to join the U.S. firm Honeywell, which was just then starting to sell its computers in Canada. He began as a computer systems engineer but quickly moved into sales where his territory was the West, "from Yonge Street to Vancouver." By 1969, he was manager of Honeywell's Toronto branch.

Then, tugged by a sentiment of nationalism that has never let go, Hutchison joined a fledgling Canadian computer company called Consolidated Computer whose research and manufacturing operations were in Ottawa. Hutchison ran the company's sales office in Toronto. Consolidated was then developing what was called a key edit system to permit the direct entry of information from a keyboard to a computer's magnetic memory, replacing the need to code it first as a pattern of holes punched into paper cards. The key edit system was ready in 1969 and became an instant international hit. Hutchison set up sales branches in the United States and Europe. Consolidated exported 90 per cent of its production, and within two years sales soared from zero to $3 million a month. Well ahead of the Japanese, Consolidated was the first foreign-based computer systems company ever to market a product in the United States. Its key edit systems were even sold in Japan itself.

Consolidated issued stock to the public in 1969, realizing what Hutchison remembers as a conscious effort by its leading figures to create a Canadian computer company. "We had all been working for multinationals, and there were enough of us who were just independent minded enough that we thought there was no reason why these products couldn't be manufactured in Canada."

Despite the technical and commercial success of the key edit system, Consolidated went into receivership in the last months of 1971. The reasons are still in dispute, but Hutchison's explanation is that its investors lost confidence in Consolidated's leadership and forced the receivership as a means of reorganizing the company's management and its financial base. Hutchison was named executive vice-president and was asked to run the place while the receiver tried to put together a plan to save it. In March 1972, the company came out of receivership and Hutchison was appointed its president under a reorganized ownership in which the Ontario and federal governments together had majority control.

The governments, as it turned out, did no better as owners even though they started with the clear objective of making Consolidated a national computer-manufacturing company. "On the one hand they were trying to take the long view, like they do in Japan," Hutchison says, "but on the other hand they wanted us to make an immediate profit." Unfortunately for Consolidated, when it was trying to bring a complete computer to production, Canada did not have a base of support firms that could supply the materials and services the company needed. "We couldn't get a printed circuit board in Canada," he says. "We used to ship our drawings down to Boston and California to get the circuit boards made for the computer. It would take us four weeks to get them. Today in Ottawa you can go down the street and get it done in twenty-four hours."

Having to import equipment was another hobble to Consolidated in its attempt to outpace the American computer makers centred in Boston and California. Importing parts meant paying duty and suffering customs delays, complains Hutchison, who remains visibly frustrated by the experience. "The government said, 'Yeah, but if you export it afterward we'll refund your money.' But in the meantime they kept the money. We had three people just filing forms for the government to get our money back."

Such exasperating redtape helps explain Hutchison's attitude. "I'm fundamentally a free trader. What we want and need most of all is free access to the American market. That's the only way any Canadian company will be successful. You should be able to build a computer in Ottawa and sell it in the United States just as easily as you could from California."

In 1975 the governments decided they wanted to sell their shares in Consolidated. The company's executives were angry because they feared the sale would destroy customer confidence, according to

Hutchison. "We said, 'Look if you want to sell it, for Christ's sake wait until we've got a stable operating business.' After our being in receivership three years earlier, a lot of people were buying from us on the confidence that the governments were backing us." In a deal that Hutchison believes had the political motive of sharing the high-tech pie between Quebec and Ontario, Ottawa sold its shares in 1976 to a Montreal company just half Consolidated's size called Central Dynamics.

Hutchison and Consolidated's top officers quit the moment the deal was signed, convinced they could not work with the Central Dynamics management. Then Central Dynamics itself became mired in financial crisis and the takeover fell apart, leaving the federal government with Consolidated still on its hands and without the executives who had been trying to make a success of it. Ultimately, Ottawa spent another $100 million on Consolidated before selling it as a derelict in 1982.

Much better success was scored by the Canadian subsidiary of a Boston company called Digital Equipment Corporation. The company had been established in 1959 in a converted woollen mill by a group of computer scientists from Massachusetts Institute of Technology. They made something called digital modules which were used to gather data for scientific experiments. The company's first Canadian customer, in 1960, was a Defence Research Board engineer named Denzil Doyle. It was a propitious sale for Digital, for Doyle, and, eventually, for Kanata.

Doyle is gruff, but a generous disposition takes cover under an exterior toughened by years of determination to be a fearless, hardheaded manager. He is an amateur genealogist and author of a book about his own family's history in the Ottawa Valley. His loyalty to the Valley is part of the explanation for Kanata's emergence as a high-tech centre. Doyle was born fifty-one years ago at Vinton, Quebec, to a family of poor farmers descended from Irish labourers brought to Canada to help build the Rideau Canal. Doyle started high school in the Ottawa Valley town of Killaloe, Ontario, and then was sent to the Jesuit Regiopolis College in Kingston. "They were going to make a priest out of me," he says. The attempt was not a success, and in 1949 Doyle quit the school with uncertain prospects. "I didn't know what I wanted to do, I just knew that I didn't want to be a priest."

He answered a newspaper advertisement inviting applications for a job as radio technician at the National Research Council and was hired "right off the farm" despite his inexperience. Then one of its lowliest employees, Doyle is today a member of the council, which directs federal government research activities across the country. He spent three years learning about radios and vacuum tubes and started a radio repair business on the side to save the money he needed to continue his education. Finally, with just enough money to cover first-year expenses, Doyle entered engineering at Queen's University in Kingston, where he paid the rest of his way by winning scholarship after scholarship, culminating in the Governor General's Medal for the highest academic average in his graduating year, 1956.

Doyle returned to the Ottawa Valley and started work with Computing Devices of Canada in Bells Corners. The company was then modifying and installing submarine detection devices for the Royal Canadian Air Force's Argus marine patrol aircraft and manufacturing computer-like equipment for the experimental reactors of Atomic Energy of Canada at Chalk River, Ontario. Doyle left Computing Devices to join the Defence Research Telecommunications Establishment, later to become the Communications Research Centre where Telidon would be invented in 1978. When Doyle came to the federal research organization in 1958, it was delving into the secrets of the ionosphere, the layer of outer atmosphere that bounces radio waves back to earth and produces the spectacle of the aurora borealis. The ionosphere is an unpredictable bouncing board for radio signals, as any shortwave listener can testify, and the Canadian military wanted its activity measured from every angle to understand it better and improve the reliability of radio communications in the north.

Doyle's job was to design some of the tests, and it was in assembling his equipment that he became the first customer in Canada for Digital Equipment's digital modules. Federal government research laboratories proved to be a lucrative market for Digital, and in 1963, the company persuaded Doyle to quit his secure government job and open a Canadian sales office for the U.S. firm. Sales boomed and very soon company management back in Massachusetts asked Doyle to start up a plant to manufacture Digital's data-gathering modules in Canada. Inspired by the parent company's example, Doyle went looking for an old woollen mill in which to set up shop. He found one west of Ottawa in Carleton Place and paid $7,000 for it.

That year, the U.S. company passed an important milestone thanks to the demands of its big Canadian customer, Atomic Energy of Canada. Digital delivered to the Crown corporation a custom-made machine that was the world's first minicomputer – not quite the desk-top size of the more recent microcomputers, but far smaller than the room-size machines then available. The minicomputer designed for Atomic Energy's Chalk River facility would turn Digital from a small successful company into a major computer maker second only to IBM in size.

By 1970, Digital Equipment of Canada had expanded into a second woollen mill in Carleton Place and was manufacturing components to be assembled into finished computers in Boston. The company had four hundred employees in Carleton Place but, says Doyle, suffered difficulties in attracting the senior engineering and managerial staff it then needed to maintain its expansion. "We agonized over the whole thing," Doyle says. "We wondered for a while whether we should go to Toronto; but we decided that we liked doing business in the Ottawa area, and we wanted to protect the jobs of those people in Carleton Place."

Those workers, most of them women, lived in the town and the surrounding countryside, and Doyle decided that the company would remain within commuting distance of their homes. And so Digital chose to relocate in Kanata where Doyle himself lived and from which he had commuted to Carleton Place. Thus, the compelling reason for Kanata's choice as the focal point of high tech in Canada is its location midway between the urban sophistication of Ottawa and the woollen mills of Carleton Place.

Digital's new plant opened in 1972 and, says Doyle, its presence was seized upon by the new local political dynamo, Marianne Wilkinson, who used Digital's move to Kanata as the foundation for a campaign to attract other well-paying, non-polluting businesses to the industrial park. "She sure exploited us every way she could," Doyle says. "Digital was not really a catalytic force, but we gave the place credibility."

The start-up of Mitel in 1973 and its frenetic growth attracted more attention to Kanata and set off the sort of chain reaction that feeds on its own energy. As more companies set up shop, more qualified engineers were attracted to Kanata, and they were in turn a magnet that drew more prospective employers. There are about

69

forty advanced technology companies in Kanata itself and 350 more in the rest of the Ottawa region. Ninety per cent of these high-tech companies are Canadian owned. Such a concentration of inventive, ambitious engineers produces a primeval broth of entrepreneurial potential from which new companies start, each seeking a niche in the evolving economy based on the microchip. Though the pattern of creation is often remarkably similar – frustrated engineers quitting jobs to start out on their own – each success has been necessarily built upon ideas that were innovative and often daring.

GANDALF: Named after the wizard of J.R.R. Tolkien's *Lord of the Rings*, Gandalf Technologies was founded with a capital of five hundred dollars by Desmond Cunningham and Colin Patterson. The inventive pair came up with an inexpensive means of transmitting computer data over local telephone lines, and "Gandalf box" has since entered the vocabulary as a generic term. Gandalf sets are also found in taxis in cities such as Ottawa and Houston, Texas, where they are linked by radio to central dispatching computers whose instructions are displayed on dashboard screens. The company also introduced one of the first systems for the connection of disparate makes of computer equipment and now is an international player with subsidiaries in the United States and Great Britain. The founders are rugged free enterprisers and have made a virtual fetish of spurning government assistance in favour of financing all research and development activity from the company's earnings.

MEMTEK: Using a process called reverse osmosis developed by the National Research Council, Memtek Corporation is mounting a high-tech attack on the old-fashioned eastern Canadian springtime. Memtek's machines filter water from maple sap without the smell of wood smoke or steamy vapours that permeate the traditional sugar bush. Memtek hopes to sell its machines in the Middle East where they would be used to extract drinking water from sea water.

EPITEK: Bell-Northern researchers Morley Miller and Jim Gardner founded Epitek Electronics in 1969 to carry on work with a process for microcircuit manufacture in which BNR had a declining interest. Sales now exceed five million dollars annually.

LUMONICS: Now the fifth-largest laser maker in the world, Lumonics began in 1981 and currently exports nearly all of its production. Lumonics lasers are used to burn code marks on products and packages.

NORPAK: Founded in 1975, Norpak has an important stake in the future of Telidon systems. It manufactures graphics display terminals and decoders that turn ordinary television sets into Telidon receivers.

CANADIAN ASTRONAUTICS: Three former Telesat Canada employees formed Canadian Astronautics in 1974 and at first worked out of their basements making satellite systems. Since then, the company has made all of the earth stations in the non-communist world's search-and-rescue satellite network and camera and antennae systems for Swedish and British satellites.

ORCATECH: While at Bell-Northern Research in the late 1970s, Ian Pearson and two other researchers completed a sophisticated computer system for the design of circuit boards. The potential uses of their computer-aided design system obviously went well beyond the in-house needs of BNR or Northern Telecom, but neither company wanted to get into the business of selling such systems to others. In an act of self-interested magnanimity, Northern sold the rights to the technology to the three in exchange for 20 per cent of their new company, Orcatech, and a promise of a 2-per-cent royalty on sales. In addition, Northern gave the new company its first substantial orders.

FOUNDATION ELECTRONIC INSTRUMENTS: Another BNR engineer, Attila Szanto, quit his job in 1977 to build custom optical fibre systems. Since then, his Foundation Electronic Instruments has produced optical fibre systems for Mexico City television stations whose copper cabling was troubled by high electrical charges emanating from the city's subway train network. The vulnerability of metal wiring to high energy pulses caused by atomic explosions has stimulated an urgent demand for optical fibre systems for military uses, and Foundation has already made field telephone systems for the Canadian Forces.

SILTRONICS: During Microsystems' inglorious demise in 1975, manager David Moore was ordered to lay off half of his department's circuit designers. Moore laid off the workers, then quit, set up Siltronics and hired some of them for his new company, which now employs fifty people in the design of custom and specialty microchips.

NABU: What may be the most innovative, daring, and least-appreciated venture in the Canadian computer and communications industries is an amalgam of home computer and cable television technology put together by a new Ottawa company called NABU Manufacturing Corporation. It is an illustration of how ideas, ambi-

71

tion, technical talent, smooth talk, and above all, the courage to take great risks combine in projects that will turn out to be either great triumphs or glorious follies. In NABU's case, the outcome is still uncertain. Technologically, at least, the NABU system of linking home computers to television cable networks that can supply a constant stream of computer programs and information is giant leaps ahead of the superficially similar Telidon. Curiously, both these systems were creations of Newfoundlanders, the NABU network originating with the company's founder and chairman, John Kelly.

NABU is the example par excellence of the effects of synergy. Kelly would not have existed as a high-tech entrepreneur nor could he have assembled his new company anywhere in Canada but in the Ottawa area. By all the measures of appearance, price, and versatility, the NABU system of using cable television channels to connect home computers to a central source of programs and information is superior to the telephone-linked videotex systems. The NABU Network could be the super-sleeper of Canadian communications technologies.

Home banking and shopping could well score major advances not with the telephone-based Telidon videotex technology but with NABU's hybrid of television cable and telephone connections. Without most people even within the communications and information industries being aware of it, NABU was developing cable-connected computer projects with Citibank Corporation of New York, which eyes its potential for home banking, and Tribune Corporation, publisher of the *Chicago Tribune*. Such banking and information organizations had been considered part of the private preserve for the marketing of Telidon systems. At the same time, NABU was slating the start-up of its first commercial home network for September 1983 in Ottawa.

NABU's threat to Telidon is unremarked, but significant. Technically, NABU Network is superior to Telidon videotex in the speed with which information is delivered to the home terminal – more than five thousand times faster than normally possible over the telephone line. A second but more important difference is that instead of transmitting information one screen at a time to a home television receiver, the NABU Network actually transmits an entire data base or program to a home computer that is sold as part of the NABU system. As operation of the program or searching of the data base does not

72

depend on two-way communication between the home terminal and the central computer, there is no limit to the number of users who can use the same program simultaneously. In addition, on the NABU system the display of text and graphic images is instantaneous, unlike the slow emergence of Telidon images.

The NABU Network transmits its programs in a repeating cycle over the cable TV line, and the person using the home computer can select, from a choice listed on his television screen, the programs or information he or she wishes to fish from the constant stream of software. Word-processing programs, educational programs, video games, restaurant reviews, and domestic financial programs are among the selections that can be electronically hooked and loaded into the NABU home computer's working memory. In May 1983 NABU accomplished a world first when it transmitted its cycle of software not by cable but by Telesat Canada's Anik D-1 satellite from Ottawa to computers exhibited at the Canadian Cable Television Association convention in Calgary. According to NABU's grand scheme, once its system is in operation on cable networks throughout North America, daily satellite links would be used to update the NABU software selection pumped out by the cable operators to subscribers' homes. Homes without cable television could also be fed the programs by direct transmissions to satellite dishes.

NABU engineers are also developing a telephone connector to be added to the NABU Personal Computer for hybrid cable-telephone communications that the company believes will be an ideal medium for some home banking and shopping operations. According to the NABU scenario, home shoppers would load an entire department store catalogue into their personal computers from the NABU cable channel. Then, no longer connected to the NABU Network, they would search for the wanted items and complete the ordering information with the guidance of a program contained within the electronic catalogue itself. When the order has been prepared to the home shopper's satisfaction – and the satisfaction of the catalogue program, which refuses impossible or incomplete requests – the shopper instructs the program to place the order. The NABU Personal Computer then automatically activates the telephone line, dials the number of the department store's computer, and in seconds transmits the order and hangs up.

73

The advantage of this shopping system over Telidon videotex is that telephone lines are not tied up for the searching session, stores can receive orders made directly to their own computers, and because the entire catalogue is contained in the home computer's own memory, the changing of pages displayed on the screen is instantaneous. With a Telidon system, by comparison, each request for a different page of the catalogue travels back down the telephone line to the central computer where it joins the queue of demands from other users of the system. The central Telidon computer then retrieves the image from its storehouse and transmits it to the shopper's home television screen. So far, Telidon has the lead in the race to become the dominant technology of home shopping and banking, not because of technological edge but because it was there first and has been adopted by the American telephone giant, AT&T, which understandably has more to gain from a telephone-based system than from John Kelly's choice of cable television as the principal medium for NABU's home communications system.

Handsome, tall, and blond, Kelly looks and sounds like actor Donald Sutherland in the 1969 film *Act of the Heart*. In that movie, set in Montreal, Sutherland played a Catholic priest tempted from his vow of chastity by a beautiful young woman, Genevieve Bujold. Kelly's own temptation was the lure of business. He was born in 1940 in St. John's, where his father was in the construction business and was campaign manager for former provincial premier Joey Smallwood. One of Kelly's two younger brothers works for NABU, but the other is a priest and vice-rector of St. Michael's Cathedral in Toronto. The Church almost captured Kelly himself, as it had nearly snared Denzil Doyle, but eventually Kelly escaped the cloth, married, and now has two children.

It was immediately after graduating from high school in Newfoundland at the age of sixteen that Kelly joined a religious teaching order called the Christian Brothers of Ireland. He was sent to study business at Iona College in New Rochelle, New York, where he won both the school's gold medal for excellence in studies of finance and the *Wall Street Journal* award for general excellence in commerce. Next he was dispatched to Montreal to teach – without pay – mathematics and English at St. Pius X High School. But when he was twenty-three, Kelly rejected both teaching and his prospective life of celibacy, poverty, and obedience and quit the Christian Brothers before taking his final vows.

He wanted instead to put into practice the business education he had acquired before going into teaching and was accepted for the three-year management training program of the Canadian Imperial Bank of Commerce. Quitting the Church, he says, was not a cataclysmic event. "It was, I guess, a heavy decision at the time, but even then it was not earth shattering. It was certainly a change of life style in terms of going from a teaching order in Montreal to Toronto and working in a bank."

All of Kelly's pay during his three years of teaching had been paid directly to the Christian Brothers. "I had a good salary when I was teaching, but I never saw any of it," he says. When Kelly left, the order gave him the hundred dollars he requested and an eighty-dollar suit. Kelly was not quite prepared for the rites of Bay Street. "I wore this single suit for the first month before I realized that people changed their suits regularly."

Though Kelly abandoned the practice along with the cloth of Catholicism, he says those seven years of his youth were well spent. "There was a certain degree of seriousness during what would normally be fairly turbulent times in one's evolution as a human being. It was disciplined. It was very intellectual and academic."

Kelly's initial contact with the computer industry came in 1967 when he was appointed assistant manager of the bank's main Ottawa branch. Here he became the personal banker for many IBM employees who were then busy selling their machines to government departments. At the time, there were few Canadian companies in the computer business, and Kelly became mesmerized by the opportunities that seemed to be emerging with the dawning computerization of society.

He quit the bank to become chief financial officer of a new firm called Alphatext, formed in 1969 to sell word-processing services before self-contained word processors had been invented. Terminals in customers' offices were connected to Alphatext's central computer. But Kelly had differences with the company's other executives and left after a year to join Leigh Instruments as corporate controller. Leigh was a publicly traded company and exposed Kelly to the stock market. But again the Newfoundlander disagreed with company financial policy and accepted a job at a new enterprise called Software-house. At the same time, he registered as a full-time student in the University of Ottawa law school. "I wanted to understand the discipline of law," Kelly says, "but I also wanted the independence of having a profession which would give me total flexibility concerning my own destiny."

Softwarehouse was a group of programmers led by Jack Davies which, after a number of transmutations, would eventually become the country's biggest software supplier, Systemhouse Limited. When Kelly joined it in 1971, Softwarehouse was strictly a small consulting company without management sophistication. Kelly's function was to impose internal discipline upon the company's operations, and he worked full time as general manager while attending law school. When Softwarehouse was purchased by a bigger computer time-sharing company called Systems Dimensions, Kelly continued to manage the new division's operations. But by 1973, the original Softwarehouse management, including Kelly, had a falling out with their parent company over the issue of whether to start writing programs for minicomputers. Systems Dimensions perceived the smaller machines, quite correctly as it turned out, to be competition to their own time-sharing business because they brought the price of computers within the reach of many of their time-sharing clients. The Softwarehouse gang advocated a different strategy, believing it wiser to get a piece of the minicomputer action than to try to ignore it. Seven of them quit in a body and formed Systemhouse. Davies and Kelly were the new company's biggest shareholders until they were joined by the man who would become the company's principal owner, president, and chairman, Rod Bryden.

Kelly was executive vice-president of Systemhouse and ran its day-to-day operations while the company grew from the original seven to six hundred employees. In 1979 Kelly decided to leave to pursue an embryonic business concept that had been developing in his mind. Kelly's scheme was to combine computers in some way with the communications power of cable television networks. It was clear to Kelly that cable television wiring and satellite transmission systems have a vast, unused capacity to deliver digital computer signals. Because of its stringy demographic pattern, with most cities just out of reach of American television signals, Canada is the most completely cabled country in the world and the leader in cable-TV technology. Eighty per cent of Canadian homes are within the reach of cable networks and 50 per cent already subscribe.

To make his entrée into the technology of cable television, Kelly sold his shares in Systemhouse and purchased control of a tiny company called Bruce Instruments located just beyond Kanata in Almonte, Ontario. Bruce Instruments, only a year old, manufactured cable television converters. Kelly assumed direct management of Bruce Instruments and convinced Mitel's Mike Cowpland to invest in the firm and share in the nurturing of his own bigger ambitions. By 1983, the converter business had become so intensely competitive that if the company were to survive, it would have had to invest millions of dollars in marketing and shift manufacturing to Asia. Deciding that the simple cable converter was a dead-end game Kelly allowed the manufacturing business to wind down while he rushed to bring his greater dream into reality.

Kelly's refined concept was the melding of people and companies with talent in microcomputers, programming, and network communications. His enthusiasm so infected two respected New York computer sages that they moved to Canada to commit themselves to the scheme. Arthur Esch, a futurist and consultant, joined Bruce Instruments to develop a marketing strategy for Kelly's idea. The other recruit was even more surprising: Citibank's top data-processing executive. John Hughes moved from a vice-presidency at Citibank to a job in Almonte, where he became chief architect of the cable-computer connection. "If leaving the Christian Brothers to join a bank was a culture shock for me, imagine what it was for John to move from Citibank in New York to Bruce Instruments in Almonte," says Kelly, in awe of his own persuasive powers.

Then he set about collecting the people and the companies he needed to realize the NABU concept, which he describes as "giving the consumers access to abundant software without forcing them into bankruptcy." His biggest convert in Kanata itself was none other than the president of Digital Equipment, Denzil Doyle, who left the company he had brought to Canada to become NABU's president. The union did not work out, but while it lasted Doyle's presence enhanced NABU's credibility with investors and potential participants in the venture.

Kelly won over the owners of the Ottawa-based Computer Innovations retail stores, a chain in which he had already invested money and which he wanted in the NABU fold both for the revenue the stores were generating and for the firm's knowledge of the microcomputer and software markets. NABU would need an inventory of programs before it could even make a demonstration of its system to cable companies and prospective subscribers, so Kelly went to see the three key owners of Mobius Software and convinced them to join NABU with their twenty-five employees. He still needed the engineering knowledge to build a new microcomputer and found it in an Ottawa firm called Andicom. Now, with Bruce Instruments well able to handle the cable television part of Kelly's concept, the parts were ready to be brought together. NABU Manufacturing Corporation came into existence on July 1, 1982, with its headquarters on the western fringe of Ottawa, a few minutes drive from downtown Kanata. Kelly came upon the name Nabu in an essay by David Godfrey in a book called *Gutenberg Two* published by Press Porcépic of Victoria, Canada's pioneer in the publishing of high-tech futurology. Nabu was the Babylonian god of writing. "Writing has been the physical communications methodology historically, and now we feel that the computer is in fact replacing writing as the primary tool for physical communication," Kelly says.

Another thing NABU needed was steady revenue to keep the company financially healthy and the investors, many of whom still don't quite understand what NABU is all about, reassured that this was in fact a business and not a wild technological fantasy. The company decided to acquire the hulk of Consolidated Computer from the federal government. Consolidated as a fount of innovative products was a dead loss, but there were still a lot of the company's successful key edit systems in the offices of customers, and their monthly lease payments were a steady source of cash, though not enough to cover Consolidated's operating losses.

NABU paid Ottawa $100,000 for the company and agreed to split the lease revenue over the next five years, a deal that Kelly estimates will give the government another six million to ten million dollars. Consolidated's greatest technical strength was its service operation, and this Kelly has decided to expand into a national network of microcomputer repair stations that will maintain not just the NABU

Personal Computer but other makes installed in homes and businesses. Consolidated's manufacturing operations have been wound down, and NABU's sleek black home computer, which resembles a stereo receiver and costs cable subscribers about a thousand dollars, is manufactured in Korea and Hong Kong. The more complex equipment for transmitting the NABU software from cable company offices will be made in Canada and the United States.

Assembling the people and the corporate bits that made up NABU had cost $9 million by the time the company was ready to begin building computers, writing programs, and designing the system by which the programs could be transmitted to homes by television cable. Of that, $500,000 was Kelly's own money, and the rest came from more than two dozen individual investors. "They were people who either believed in me or believed in the concept," Kelly says. "Sometimes I'm not sure which." With the initial investment exhausted in bringing the elements together, NABU resorted to bank loans to finance its research drive while it prepared a private stock offering to raise the capital it would need to carry through its ambitious plan, fraught with unknown technological and marketing risks.

The private placement, handled by broker Wood Gundy in the autumn of 1981, raised $17 million. As a result of that investment, Kelly's personal share of NABU was reduced to 5 per cent. Other 5-per-cent stakes are held by Investors Syndicate, the Saskatchewan government's Crown Investment Corporation, and Bytec. The biggest single shareholder, with 10 per cent, is Kanata's real estate and development master, Campeau Corporation, which decided that it wanted in on the high-tech prosperity it saw all around it in Kanata. In December 1982 NABU became a publicly traded company and raised a further $25 million in its initial offering of shares on the Toronto Stock Exchange. Kelly estimates that the NABU concept will have cost $20 million in research and development before it becomes commercially viable.

Kelly lost one of his most reassuring assets in 1982 when Denzil Doyle quit the NABU presidency. Doyle says he left because he found the cable television side of the NABU project to be beyond his experience. It was also difficult, he says, to work with executives and managers he had not personally hired, as he had every senior person at Digital. Doyle has set up shop as a private consultant in a modest office building on Carling Avenue in Kanata with his daughter as office manager and receptionist. It is, he says, much like the one-room office he opened as Digital Equipment's Canadian branch twenty years earlier, and through his window he can look directly across the road to the spreading Digital Equipment complex, now employing more than a thousand people, that he brought to Kanata. Doyle's ambition now is to create other Kanatas in regions where there is potential for synergistic growth of high-tech clusters but where entrepreneurialism and capitalism have yet to fuse in a self-sustaining chain reaction.

He says he was a "grandfather" to many of Kanata's young engineer-entrepreneurs, to whom he refers as "the kids." Kanata, according to Doyle, "is an accident which can be repeated." He wants "free run of the land to locate people who are working on research that could lead to a commercial venture." Doyle points to Halifax as a city ticking with potential to explode as a centre of advanced technology enterprise. The city's oceanographic and defence research laboratories and the facilities of the national and Nova Scotia research councils are rich with innovations that, if they could be combined with the "old money" Doyle believes is mouldering in the bank accounts of Nova Scotia's established families, would fuel a strong local industry.

His immediate preoccupation, however, is Saskatoon, which seems the most likely of any Canadian city to rival Kanata in its technological effervescence. Enough high-tech industry is already in place to have merited the pleasant prairie city the title "Silicon Flats." Northern Telecom has made Saskatoon its world centre for the manufacture of optical fibres, with the incentive of the Saskatchewan government's decision in 1980 to install 3,200 kilometres of optical cable.* The city also has an important installation of AEL Microtel of

---

*Optical fibre is made of silicon and carries pulses of light generated by tiny lasers. One strand of optical fibre can carry twenty thousand simultaneous telephone calls. Optical switches are now being developed and it is reasonable to anticipate that computers will eventually run not on electricity but on beams of light. In 1983, Bell-Northern Research opened the first building in Edmonton's Research and Development Park, where it will concentrate its work in fibre optics. Optical fibre may destroy copper mining in Canada since the replacement of existing cabling will produce an abundance of copper which could be recycled.

80

Vancouver and the academic assets of the University of Saskatchewan, which was enlightened enough in 1972 to make a private enterprise of its space engineering division. Today a company of three hundred employees, SED Systems sells everything from satellite components to agricultural instruments that can electronically monitor the operation of combines to reduce grain loss during the wheat harvest. Another firm, Develcon Electronics, has in just five years become what the computer industry calls a "world-class" supplier of computer communications equipment to markets in the United States and Europe. Saskatoon, says Doyle, has the "technology engine" to drive another Kanata.

In 1983 Saskatchewan hired Doyle to add financial wheels to that technological engine. His mandate is to scour the province's research laboratories for projects with commercial potential and then teach "the kids" who created them how to start a business. Doyle is then to become a marriage broker between the new entrepreneurs and venture capitalists. Except among its farmers, Saskatchewan lacks enough entrepreneurs and risk-taking capitalists to match its scientific assets.

To infect with the capitalist ethic a province perhaps too sanctimonious in its tradition of populist socialism, Saskatchewan's Conservative government has retained another Kanatan, Brian Beninger, whose specialty is money. Beninger is president of the venture capital firm Kanata Genesis Fund and is advising the Saskatchewan government in the drafting of legislation to create a channel for private money into high-risk high-tech businesses. Investors in Beninger's Kanata Genesis Fund get directly from the Ontario government a tax-free cash grant equal to 30 per cent of their investment. Beninger believes the prairie province should adopt similar legislation to entice local money into high technology. "We're suggesting that Saskatchewan grow its own venture capitalists," Beninger says.

There are other Canadian cities that can be classed as high-tech clusters. Bromont in Quebec's picturesque Eastern Townships is home not only to Mitel's main microchip factory but also to an IBM plant which makes computer parts and electric typewriters. Montreal is, in part because of its linguistic difference, the major world centre of word-processing innovation. Both AES Data and Micom are based in the city along with Laurent Nadeau's Comterm. It is also the home of the world's leading producer of the automatic soldering equipment that is used by every major microelectronics manufacturer in the world. The company, Electrovert, was founded in 1952 by an immigrant from Hungary named Nicholas Fodor. Now a vigorous seventy-nine years old, his head crowned with thick, cloud-white hair, Fodor relinquished daily control of his firm only in 1983 after building a one-man importing business into a major exporter of its own equipment to seventy countries. Electrovert now has plants in Canada, the United States, and Ireland. Its "wave" soldering machines freeze into place the pins of the dozens of microchips and other components protruding through the bottoms of circuit boards. The boards skim the crest of an elongated ridge of molten solder, their pins just dipping into the hot metal.

In Ontario, Brockville has an important AEL Microtel plant and the country's biggest contract circuit board maker, Computer Assembly Systems. The ten-year-old firm uses automatic machines to insert microchips and other components into green printed circuit boards and then wave-solders everything in place in one smooth pass. Linear Technology of Burlington is Canada's only contract designer and manufacturer of microchips and exports nearly all of its production to the United States, Europe, and Asia. Kitchener is the headquarters of Canadian-owned Electrohome, which beginning in 1907 manufactured phonographs, then made living-room hi-fi's and colour televisions, and now is a major supplier of Telidon screens and colour video display monitors for computers. Also in Kitchener is the oddly named dAVID Computers, which produces microcomputers for the business market.

The Toronto suburbs of Mississauga, Markham, and Don Mills are the preferred lairs of the multinational computer companies, but they also shelter a number of smaller, Canadian-owned firms that have successfully laid claim to a share of the computer market. GEAC Computers International supplies computer hardware and software for library and banking needs. Nelma Data Corporation manufactures both a successful and low-cost microcomputer called the Persona and the world's first system that lets computers communicate with each other by radio instead of cables. Lanpar Technologies manufactures both computer terminals of its own design and Osborne personal computers for the Canadian market.

Downtown Toronto's high-tech strength is in the creative application of computing power. I.P. Sharp Associates is one of the world's biggest suppliers of computer power and information, distributed over its own international network. Teleride/Sage is the marriage of the two North American leaders in the computerization of mass transit. Bus and driver scheduling for Toronto, Washington, Chicago, Miami, and Ottawa have all been done by the company's computers in downtown Toronto, connected by telephone lines to each city's transit system offices. Sage was established in 1968 by Ian Moore when he was with IBM in Montreal and was originally a private investment system that used a computer model to detect tell-tale fluctuations in stock prices indicating that stock speculators were driving up the price of certain shares. Moore would then buy the rising stock. The system had an unfortunate flaw. "What it didn't tell us was when to sell the suckers," laments Moore, who is now Teleride/Sage marketing director.

President of Teleride/Sage is Josef Kates, who fled his native Vienna as a child in 1938 to escape the Nazis. Kates arrived at Quebec City in 1940 with a shipload of German-speaking refugees whom the Allies treated with distrust because they feared the presence of enemy agents among them. For two years, Canadian authorities kept Kates and his fellow refugees interned in camps where the older men among them assumed responsibility for teaching the children. Their educational supplies were donated books and toilet paper to write on. From his internment camp classroom, Kates wrote the McGill University senior matriculation examination and came first among all the high school students in Quebec who took the examination. "I was quite mediocre before that," he recalls. "Motivation is everything."

Kates studied mathematics and physics at the University of Toronto, and though he had not studied a single course in engineering he wrote and passed the professional engineers' exam after studying the subject on his own. In 1948, he went to work for the university's new computing centre and built Bertie the Brain, the world's first electronic games computer, which played tic-tac-toe for visitors to the Canadian National Exhibition in 1951. Kates was also the brain behind the university's full-scale prototype computer called UTEC – which some computer pioneers believe could have made Canada a leader in big computers had the university and its federal government sponsors paid for its refinement. Instead, in 1952, they purchased a Ferranti computer made in England and the Canadian machine was scrapped. Kates turned from computer hardware to software and in 1953 designed the first computerized seat reservation system for TransCanada Airlines. This was Kates's first transportation project.

As a private consultant Kates began to specialize in transportation, and much of Toronto's highway and mass transit network was laid out according to his computer simulations of future traffic patterns. Toronto traffic lights are also controlled by a Kates-designed system that uses sensors buried in the roadway to monitor the speed and density of traffic. Kates was chairman of the Science Council of Canada from 1975 to 1978 and then returned to business, determined to enhance the attractiveness of public transit systems. Teleride was the result, and now riders in ten North American cities, including Toronto, Ottawa, San Diego, and Salt Lake City, can call a computer to learn the next scheduled arrival at their stop. Ridership has increased significantly in every case, says Kates. "The reason people don't like the bus is not the bus – it's the wait." The most sophisticated of Teleride's systems employ electronic odometers on each bus to measure its precise progress along the route. The bus's location is radioed every thirty seconds to the central computer, which calculates how long it will take for each vehicle to reach its next stop.

In the Vancouver area, MacDonald Dettwiler and Associates is the world's leading supplier of ground stations for weather satellites. The computer science department of the University of British Columbia supplies a strong software sector with talented programmers. Sydney Development Corporation is the best known of the local program producers, as much for its creative financing schemes as for its products. Basic Software Group was created by a group of UBC computer science graduates and markets a highly successful series of microcomputer programs. Most of the firm's client computer companies are based in the southwestern states. "We understand California's way of doing business," says Basic Software Group vice-president Norm Francis. "Toronto is three time zones away. San Francisco is two hours from here on the same time."

Still, the West Coast is poor in high-technology industry considering the attraction its climate, outdoor life, and psychological proximity to California should have for engineers and entrepreneurs. The provincial government is struggling hard to remedy the situation but has perhaps missed the lesson of synergy by spreading its resources too widely across the province. British Columbia is attempting to nurture simultaneously four synthetic high-tech clusters in the province when past patterns of the industry's growth indicate that it might be wiser to focus on one, at least at first. And British Columbia is not alone in stretching its high-tech resources almost into attenuation. Ottawa and most of the provincial governments have been unable to resist the temptation to turn the new technologies into old-fashioned pork barrels by trying to spread facilities all across their jurisdictions, thereby unwittingly ensuring that synergy will not take hold.

The first of British Columbia's so-called Discovery Parks is located on Burnaby Mountain, where AEL Microtel has opened its new research centre. Though AEL Microtel is, through its immediate parent, British Columbia Telephone Company, a subsidiary of the U.S. General Telephone & Electronics Corporation, the province hopes Microtel Pacific Research will be the BNR of British Columbia. Heart of the research establishment is an advanced microchip design facility which is Microtel's contribution to a unique transnational consortium of universities and private companies in Washington, Oregon, and British Columbia dedicated to transferring the results of high-tech research to industry. As part of the consortium deal, any British Columbia university or company may use the centre's facilities to design special microchips.

The chip design centre is managed by forty-four-year-old Alberta-born engineer Paul Thiel, who says the use of computer-aided design to create microchips is an extension of the mind the way computer-aided drafting is an extension of the hand. Using the usual current methods, a chip designer writes a "truth table," which is basically a check-list of what the chip is required to do. "If there are no cars coming this way and there are cars coming this way and if there are three cars here and five there, what should it do?" is Thiel's illustration of how logic is programmed into a slice of silicon. An engineer in circuit design then sits down with a ruler and pencil and translates the truth table into a pattern of electrical pathways and gates. Finally, a draftsman makes the detailed plans from which the chip itself is fabricated.

With the automated system at the Pacific Research Centre, the chip designer enters the truth table at a computer keyboard and, without anyone touching pencil to paper, the computer produces a final coloured drawing of the circuitry. Even this illustration is really unnecessary because the computer also controls the chip-making process itself in microchip plants called foundries. Microtel's own chips are made in Arizona using a process its parent company purchased from Mitel for $1.5 million.

There is no central brain in a microchip. Its functions are controlled by the logic programmed into it by its human designer. Though British Columbia now has the latest gear for chip design, what counts is the brain power that will use it. British Columbia's future in high-technology enterprise is not guaranteed by the province's usual inventory of natural resources. A high-tech cluster is like a microchip. It doesn't depend on a central authority but relies instead on the diffuse intelligence of a network. "Our biggest resource is our people," says Thiel. "If you only have two or three people who are knowledgeable, you've got a problem. What we have to do is attain a critical mass of enough people who can help each other. Kanata has done a terrific job, and if we want to live out here in British Columbia and have something for our children to do, then we have to get going now."

CHAPTER FOUR

The Prophet Motive

If Kanata and most of Canada's other nascent microelectronics clusters are, as Denzil Doyle claims, just happy accidents, there is in Montreal a concentration of high-tech talent and success created by a single man once driven by a personal vendetta. But that man is just about as friendly a guy as one could meet. Tall, lanky, curly-headed, blessed by an irrepressible grin, Stephen Dorsey is remarkably open about the fears, the angers, and the satisfactions that came in unending rushes during his journey from restless youth to wealth and recognition. At the age of forty-five, Dorsey is the world's leading innovator in the design and manufacture of word processors.

Though the unfortunate designation "word processor" is an offence to language itself, the application of computer technology in the invention of a new writing machine may be, more than anything else, what made the advantages of microelectronics understandable and clearly useful to most of us. Little computers are just as good at the manipulation of words as of numbers, and it's not until a typist or writer has experienced the relaxation of working with these machines that he or she realizes just how much sheer drudgery, physical and emotional, goes into old-fashioned typing to paper.

Dorsey built not one but two international leaders among manufacturers of word processors, and both, from their Montreal headquarters and factories, successfully staked out shares of the world market while feuding with each other. Today AES Data and Micom Company sell their machines around the globe, and each is working feverishly to bring keyboards and screens to the executive desk as they and just about every other company in the office machine business move towards the paperless office. Word processors in the typing pool were the thin edge of the electronic wedge. The machines meant for secretaries and typists have now evolved into telecommunications terminals capable of sending documents down phone lines to anywhere in the world while their executive versions are used to compose and deliver messages that traditionally consumed paper or time on the telephone.

Along his uneven road to success, Dorsey concluded that corporate "culture" is as important as financial clout in the choice of business associates. He acquired an abiding gratitude for the willingness of government officials to take chances on new Canadian products. Dorsey has also accumulated a set of resentments at some Canadian financial institutions, notably banks and venture capitalists. In its hours of crisis, Canadian banks and capitalists took his first company, AES, away from him. And later, in time of need and opportunity, it was foreign-based lenders and investors who made Dorsey's second firm, Micom, a success.

Despite its success and sales throughout the world, Micom's rented executive offices are located in a utilitarian building amid one of Canada's ugliest industrial agglomerations, which spreads like an oil slick outward from the intersection of the Trans-Canada Highway and the fumy pit of the sunken Décarie Expressway. Blue Bonnets Raceway, an all-day strip bar, the grotesque translucent sphere of an Orange Julep stand, and the outlandishly huge Ruby Foo's and Bill Wong's restaurants make the area a disaster zone of aesthetic taste. But their location in the predominantly French-speaking city also meant that AES and Micom, from the start, had to produce machines with keyboards, screens, and software that would function in more than one language. Dorsey's companies thus gained an advantage over the big American word processor makers IBM and Wang in the penetration of foreign markets. Micom now makes versions of its word processor for fourteen different languages.

Dorsey was born in Montreal in 1937 and has lived most of his life since in the solid, expensive enclave of Westmount. His father, Louis, a lawyer, opened a clothing factory and subsequently switched from soft goods to hardware when he bought a small machine shop which did made-to-order work for customers with needs that couldn't be satisfied by commonly available hardware. By chance, the Dorsey machine shop was asked by one customer to produce a large set of big bolts and that first experience with manufacturing in series inspired the senior Dorsey to turn his little atelier into a full-scale manufacturing operation called Industrial Screw and Machine Works.

One of the young Dorsey's early passions, meanwhile, was amateur radio, and he was a licensed ham by the age of twelve – the second youngest in Canada. The Dorsey backyard on Roslyn Avenue was webbed with Stephen's antennae, attached through his bedroom window to the transmitters he built from scratch. Dorsey's fascination with amateur radio began when he saw the set-up belonging to the son of a radio repairman. Dorsey remembers, "He had wall to wall equipment with blue tubes and meters flying and everything else. I said, 'I've got to do that.'"

The love affair with electronics endured, and Dorsey entered the faculty of engineering at McGill University, only to suffer disenchantment. He had envisaged engineering as a discipline of thought and theory, but McGill, in 1954, was still stuck in traditions of steel and concrete. "An engineer had to be a surveyor. He had to wear a slide rule in his belt. He had to drink beer and wear a red jacket. None of those things appealed to me," Dorsey recalls. So, after one year at McGill, he applied for admission to the more prestigious Massachusetts Institute of Technology. Dorsey's life is starred with strokes of happy accident. One of those minor events with major consequences helped him gain admittance to MIT. Letters of recommendation were as important to MIT as Dorsey's A average. Dorsey's application was accompanied by a testimonial from his high school principal who considered Dorsey to be a wizard in electronics.

After dozens of unsuccessful attempts by experts to repair Westmount High School's broken public address system, the principal was desperate. Dorsey recalls, "He had heard that I was a radio amateur and he called me in to see if I could fix it." Dorsey squeezed into the PA system's control cabinet to have a look. "I guess maybe because I was more agile or something, I happened to see a wire that looked loose and put it back in place. Word got out that I was a genius."

In Boston, MIT authorities wanted Dorsey to start from scratch in first year because his McGill studies had not included calculus. Instead, Dorsey bought the course textbook and returned to Montreal for a week of intense study. He returned to Boston, passed a special oral exam and was admitted to second-year engineering. Dorsey graduated from MIT in 1958, well before the invention of the microchip and before computers were a part of the engineering curriculum, with ambitions no better defined than when he entered. "I didn't have any burning sense of direction," he says. He returned to Montreal and started work at CAE Electronics, maker of the world's most sophisticated flight simulators for the training of jet pilots. Dorsey, however, wasn't excited by the job. "I did some obscure work on amplifiers. I wasn't super impressed with myself."

Restless, in 1960 Dorsey applied for and got one of the French government's generous work-and-study scholarships for foreigners. He went to work as a visiting student at Compagnie Générale TSF, the research subsidiary of the French telephone system. Again, he had only moderate interest in the job. "I worked the minimum number of hours I could. I was just more interested in seeing Paris and visiting the galleries than I was turned on by the technology," he says. "I felt a need to complement my technical background and, as I usually do, I became obsessed with one thing, this time the study of art and architecture."

At the end of his eight-month program, Dorsey encountered another of the happy surprises that have redirected his life. He was called into the administrative office of his employer and handed a cheque equal to eight months' pay, despite the fact that he had been getting $150 every month from the French government. Dorsey still isn't sure why he was paid twice but believes that French law prevented the company from using the results of his work unless it had paid for it.

Unexpectedly rich, in student terms, Dorsey headed for Greece in his Peugeot. From there he shipped his car to Israel, where he motored about the country for four months. Spoiled by the superb guide books of France, Dorsey was disappointed at Israel's poverty of tourist information and decided to write his own guide to the country. "No one had done a proper book on Israel. That was a lot of fun. I got a lot of it put together and went to New York to try to find a publisher. I found one who was all set to make a deal with me when a competing book came out written by the wife of the Israeli ambassador to the United Nations. That was probably the luckiest thing that

90

ever happened to me, otherwise I might be a writer today." Dorsey now finds writing "a painful process," and he dictates his business correspondence. Ironically, the inventor of the world's most advanced word processors doesn't write with one. "I've taken a typing course, but I'm not very good," he says a bit sheepishly. The terminal behind his desk is used to keep track of Dorsey's business agenda and electronic mail messages.

Though it saved him from the ruination of a writing career, the sinking of his venture as an author left Dorsey searching once more for new direction. "I wasn't sure that I would be good as an engineer. I didn't have the greatest confidence.

"My father asked me if I'd like to work for him, so I went into Industrial Screw and Machine Works and got interested in selling. I learned a lot about selling from my father. When you are selling nuts and bolts and screws, your nuts and bolts and screws aren't any better than anybody else's, so the real knack is to develop skills of dealing with people, getting them to like you."

After a year, Dorsey came to the conclusion that no matter how good the relationship between father and son, joining the family business strains both family and business. "I started to feel that this wasn't good for him or for me. On the other hand, I had no financing, so he started me off on my own with what we called the Automatic Systems Division of Industrial Screw and Machine Works. He just lent me the money to do it."

It was now 1965 and Dorsey had his own business, with a little office in his father's plant on Paré Street, in the same industrial neighbourhood where he works today. All he needed then was customers and something to sell to them. "I don't even know how I got started because I had no products. I just went out and started calling on accounts, believe it or not, trying to find out what I could sell in Canada." Once more, Dorsey's luck intervened, this time to turn someone else's error into his entrée to opportunity. "I went into CP Telecommunications and introduced myself to a nice elderly gentleman. At first he thought that I was from another, well-known company called Automatic Electric, and he said he was looking for little remote control systems for microwave radio stations. I immediately found out that I could buy such systems from a company in the United States. I bought them, painted them a different colour, and sold them to CP." The CP order was worth $15,000, and Dorsey's business was underway.

Dorsey next learned that CP Telecommunications had a contract from the federal government for the installation of more sophisticated remote control systems to monitor radio relay stations, which pick up and pass on microwave signals. Getting the specifications for the system from CP, the young entrepreneur pulled together a small group of engineers who designed and assembled the boxes in six months. "We made only one error. The plug-in boards were so close together that they constantly shorted each other, and we had a lot of trouble with it. I was very nervous about how well the system would work. Fortunately we got a break. The government cancelled the microwave project and the equipment was put in a warehouse and never installed."

Though, mercifully, that first system was not tried in the field, Dorsey's engineering group, which had grown to twenty people, had gained a lot of experience with remote monitoring systems, and the little company started to bid for business with power utilities and telephone companies which used radio systems to control their networks. The systems had to be extremely reliable and capable of operating in an environment polluted with electromagnetic charges, which can confuse electronic equipment the way a vacuum cleaner, for example, can interfere with a radio. He says, looking back, "I started to get keen on engineering again. I really enjoyed the technology. I had very little interest, unfortunately, in money or the administrative side of the business. I got my kicks building bigger and better boxes."

Dorsey's private life was also succeeding nicely. As he was starting his business in 1965, Dorsey fell in socially with a group of young architects enjoying Montreal's boom of creative building leading up to the Expo 67 world's fair. One of them, Tanja Hahn of Vancouver, was working on architect Moshe Safdie's Habitat apartment complex built in the midst of the port area. Stephen and Tanja married and have since raised a family of five children in a 120-year-old house in Westmount that Tanja had renovated according to her plans. Tanja is now designing a new house the couple are planning to build up the hill from their present home.

Renamed Automatic Electronic Systems, Dorsey's company had become legally independent of his father's business, but in reality it still depended on the older man's generosity. The new enterprise was generating more than a million dollars in annual business, an impressive performance had it not been for the fact that it was supported by continued infusions of Dad's cash. Dorsey recalls, "My father started to get in deeper and deeper. Finally he said, 'That's it.'" In addition, his father urged him to follow the example of his own firm and develop a product that could be made in series and marketed in mass.

Dorsey accepted this advice. He asked his engineers to put together a system that could be sold to power utilities everywhere. Dorsey's Tele-Protection device was designed to work on the few occasions when a power line fails. Using a telephone circuit, it sends a tone to the closest substation where it activates a circuit breaker and cuts the faulty line from the power grid. The device was sold to power utilities across North America. "We developed probably the only system in the world that never failed," says Dorsey. "That became a real cash cow. It was the first taste of the joys of product and it put us on the map."

With the security of steady revenue generated by the Tele-Protection device, Dorsey and his engineers mulled over ways to improve the product. At that time, the operation of such electronic devices was controlled by the pattern of the wiring joining their internal components. The machine had only one function and to modify its operation meant creating a new circuit board. For this reason the device could not be adapted to new tasks without abandoning the advantages of mass production. In the late 1960s, experimenters were toying with circuits whose functions could be directed by signals stored within programmable microchips rather than by physical changes in the circuits. These experimental devices were called microprocessors, though they were still big compared with current versions that reside on a single chip.

"We made one of the first three commercial microprocessors in North America," Dorsey says. "We made ours by putting about fifty chips together on a board, but it did the same thing that the one-chip microprocessor does today. This opened a whole new world because it now allowed us to start doing things with software."

Dorsey quickly realized that his microprocessor could be used in all sorts of products completely unrelated to his own company's power utility control devices. Automatic Electronic Systems sold its microprocessor to other electronics firms, including one that bought a thousand units for a system to control traffic lights in Baltimore. Dorsey also tried but failed to interest a pioneering U.S. maker of word-processing equipment in using his microprocessor. This sales attempt did, however, give Dorsey a peek at the nascent word-processing technology, which was then little more than the storage of typed texts on magnetic cards. He became convinced by his own sales pitch that the microprocessor was the key to success in word processing because with it the machines could be flexible and could be improved by changes in software.

Dorsey mobilized a team of six engineers to work for a year under his personal authority on the design of a word processor with a microprocessor at its heart. In 1972 the company introduced the world's first programmable word processor with a video screen. But the real breakthrough by Dorsey's AES team was that their machine stored the operator's texts on magnetic disks. Texts could be retrieved from the disks simply by entering their names at the keyboard. It was actually a sophisticated microcomputer that could be reprogrammed by changing the instructions contained within a few chips. "The programmability really put it a whole generation ahead of the others," Dorsey says. "It meant we could constantly improve the features of the equipment, even after it was already installed in a customer's office."

Dorsey started selling his word processor even before it was anything more than an idea and a set of crude circuit layouts called breadboards. "Our first order came from Air Canada and the second was from the Department of National Defence. They came in and saw a breadboard spread over the whole table and they said that was exactly what they wanted. They bought our first units and started us off in the government."

Once the machine – the AES 90 – was in production, Dorsey recruited small sales teams in Montreal and Ottawa. They included some salesmen lured away from IBM by the quality of the new word processor and the excitement of a new venture, which was what AES had in essence become with its audacious attempt to penetrate the market for expensive office machines. At the time, that market was ruled by IBM, which rented its equipment to customers. That practice forced IBM's competitors to offer similar leasing arrangements. IBM, of course, could afford to delay recovery of the cost of its equipment for several years while smaller competitors had to find financing companies willing to lease the machines to customers.

AES found a lease financier in a subsidiary of the Royal Bank of Canada called RoyMarine Leasing, which agreed to pay AES for every machine it installed under a leasing arrangement. AES would get somewhat less than the total leasing price to the customer, and RoyMarine would take over collection of the monthly payments. The deal seemed to be set, and the company's prospects, at the start of 1974, appeared to be golden. Dozens of AES word processors were functioning well in customers' offices; orders for more were piling up at the plant. Then, in Dorsey's words, "everything hit the fan." The leasing company's parent, the Royal Bank, decided to nix the leasing deal. AES already owed the Royal $500,000, and the bank had little confidence that a small company operating in Montreal could successfully stake out a place in the computer market.

Just weeks after refusing AES access to lease financing, the Royal Bank walked in with a receiver and took over the management from Dorsey, threatening to force bankruptcy upon him. "That started probably the two most horrendous months I've ever spent," Dorsey says. "I had to try to keep up the morale of the people, saying we were going to solve this thing one way or the other." In the weeks before the bank moved in, Dorsey had been trying to attract outside investment in AES. Northern Telecom was offered but declined a substantial share in AES, a refusal that Dorsey now finds ironic, given the millions Northern has spent since trying to catch up in office technology. The Canadian subsidiary of the Dutch multinational Philips also refused to invest. "The story we heard over and over again," Dorsey says, "was, 'Look, there have been no high-tech successes in Canada. Why do you think you can do it?'"

As AES teetered on the edge of bankruptcy, Dorsey learned to cope with personal stress and public embarrassment. "I lost about fifteen pounds. I made more difficult decisions in a day than one would normally make in a month. I had to make decisions on bluff and all sorts of bloody things." Dorsey decided even then that the crisis would be no more than "a glitch in the career." He would not let the

AES crisis crush his ambition. "You have to have a hell of an ego to say that stuff doesn't count, that it doesn't mean a damn thing," he says.

Dorsey was desperate enough to attempt to attract the interest of venture capitalists, the horned angels of hard-pressed entrepreneurs. Venture capitalists provide money to young companies that are rich in prospects but short of cash. They expect, however, to get returns of 30 to 40 per cent a year on their investments and often demand control of ownership and management. If the entrepreneur fails to deliver on his promises of high profits, they force him out.

One of the venture capital firms Dorsey invited in to look at AES was Innocan Investments, owned by the Canada Development Corporation and a group of banks. Innocan said it wasn't interested, but Dorsey now believes Innocan was in fact behaving like a vulture capitalist, waiting for its wounded prey to die before swooping down for an easy meal. "I am absolutely convinced that Innocan just waited for us to go broke so that they could buy at a bargain basement price instead of coming in earlier when the company was still viable. When things really got bad they suddenly got interested."

With the end of AES at hand and Dorsey apparently without a shred of bargaining power left, Innocan entered the scene with an offer to take over AES with an investment of $500,000 in new working capital. Dorsey would be left no share in ownership or management. "There was an incredible weekend which I'll never forget," says Dorsey. "Innocan called me in on a Friday and they had a whole thing for me to sign right away. It gave me zero equity. Even though the banks were pressuring me to make a deal at any cost, and probably could have forced me to do it, I just said, 'No deal. I've got an offer from the Quebec government. I'm going to go with it because I don't like the way you people operate.'"

Dorsey's exaggerated claim of a better deal with the provincial government forced Innocan into retreat. "I really didn't have a firm deal with Quebec, but I just didn't want to go with them. In any case, Innocan phoned me on Tuesday to say that they'd changed their mind and saw my point of view and offered me a 25-per-cent equity. I signed because I didn't really know whether the Quebec deal would come through or not. Anyway, my bluff worked. I got some equity."

The deal also allowed Dorsey to stay on as president of AES, but that did nothing to alleviate the hostility that had built up between Dorsey and Innocan during their negotiations. What made the Innocan negotiations seem all the bloodier to Dorsey was that Innocan's agent, Paul Lowenstein, had been a childhood friend. "They didn't want me to be president, but I was already thinking of the next company because I didn't like them at all. I felt that it would be important, when people asked me what I did, to be able to say I was president of AES. Innocan just thought I had an ego problem. So I stayed as president while they in fact ran the company."

What Dorsey the nominal president did was establish a sales office in Toronto and sell AES word processors on commission, a task he assigned to himself because it was a way to learn at first hand what customers wanted from a word processor. "I had no experience selling door to door. I wanted to really see what it took to sell this product to a real end-user. I became a hell of a salesman." For ten months, Dorsey sold AES word processors by day and planned his next venture by night. One of his rare attempts as president to influence the course of AES was a campaign to have the company's engineers use the Intel single-chip microprocessor which, by replacing dozens of microchips with one, would have made the word processor smaller and less expensive to build. But the AES engineers were committed to improving their own multi-chip microprocessor, and Dorsey was without the power to impose his views.

Innocan had hired a chief executive officer named Walter Steele to wield the real power at AES. Steele and Dorsey quickly warred. "I came back one weekend from a business trip to Toronto and discovered that he had decided my office was better. So all my stuff was piled in a corner in his old office. I figured I had to get out. But I just didn't know how." Steele and Innocan felt the same way about Dorsey, and a week after being evicted from his old office Dorsey overheard Steele say that he would like the company to buy Dorsey's shares and force him out. Dorsey decided to hasten the dénouement. "As soon as I heard that I consulted with a lawyer, who said, 'Look, you have to be constructive, but the more unpleasant you can be in a constructive way the better.'" With that strategy as his guide, Dorsey began to involve himself with an increasing share of AES management. "I treated Walter as if he worked for me. I'd order him into my office and in meetings I'd criticize him. Normally, I wouldn't treat anyone the way I tried to treat him. He couldn't stand me, and I knew that both he and Lowenstein were plotting how to get me out. Which is exactly what I wanted.

"Finally they came and said they were willing to make an offer for my shares. We made a deal for a nominal amount compared to what the company was worth, but for me it was an absolute relief to get away from there." Dorsey was paid $135,000 to quit AES, and Innocan wanted him to sign a promise that he would not start a competing business, a condition that Dorsey flatly refused. "I said that if I wasn't good enough to run AES they shouldn't be afraid of me when they had Xerox, IBM, and everybody else to contend with."

At the end of his unhappy separation from his first business, Dorsey felt cheated less of money than of time. "The only thing that I felt was unrecoverable was holidays, of all things. I had missed all those holidays with my family and then this thing happened anyway. So I made an absolute rule that I would have holidays for the rest of my business career, come what may." In March 1975, Dorsey took his $135,000, paid some debts, put the rest in the bank, and flew to Bermuda for ten days.

Within a week of his return, Dorsey was back in the word-processing business with a new firm he called Micom Data Systems. He and a friend named Louis Miller established a partnership on a handshake. Miller offered Micom cheap space in the attic above his Superior Business Machines offices in a stone building in Montreal's old quarter, where the financial district meets the port (the building had been the first YMCA in North America). Access to Micom's attic was by means of a decrepit and cantankerous freight elevator. Miller also supplied office equipment and the initial components Dorsey needed to put together a prototype word processor. The proceeds of Dorsey's AES shares went to pay the salaries of four engineers.

Micom's first eight weeks were devoted to day-long brainstorming sessions whose purpose was to decide just what a perfect word processor should do. This new word processor was to be built around the Intel microprocessor refused by the engineers at AES. Dorsey had promised his wife that he would spend no more than $60,000 developing the new machine. He would, in fact, eventually sink $195,000 of savings and new borrowings into the project. Dorsey remembers Micom's infancy with nostalgia. "It was a very exciting time because business is always pure and conceptual when there are no invoices," he says. "Real business only starts when your first invoice goes out. So it was fun to be in the development mode again."

The first Micom word processor, called the Micom 2000, was shipped in July 1976. Sticking to his resolve to make family vacations a priority, Dorsey went ahead with holiday plans anyway and was on his way to Maine the day the machine left the attic plant. "I was on the phone two hours a day to see if we were still in business, but I said, 'Dammit, I'm taking holidays.'" Upon his return, Dorsey started calling on potential clients, some of whom already had AES machines. He wanted above all to make some money for Micom. But he also wanted to prove to AES that it had erred in pushing him aside. By his own account, "It really was a personal vendetta. I felt that a company like Innocan, which was funded by Canadian government money, should have had an entirely different attitude towards entrepreneurs than they did. They didn't have to be the all-out bastards that they were. They could have looked at it equitably. I was a big boy. I knew I'd have to give up shares. We might have all been still working together today."

Dorsey's antagonist at AES, Paul Lowenstein, invited Dorsey to breakfast one day and declared that AES would put Micom out of business. Instead of accepting healthy competition, the two Montreal word processor makers locked horns in a vicious, private war. Walter Steele of AES, according to Dorsey, couldn't stand crossing paths with his rival at trade shows. "My style was always to pretend nothing had happened, to just say, 'How are you Walter?' He'd walk away to avoid shaking hands."

Dorsey was warmed by the renewed confidence of old clients and even of suppliers who had never recovered all they were owed by AES. Not a single supplier refused credit to Micom. In its first year of production, Micom shipped two million dollars' worth of machines from its little shop in the attic at a rhythm of fifteen a month.

In March 1977, Micom got what Dorsey considers the big break that often determines the success of start-up companies, which otherwise might wither before flowering. The Department of Supply and Services had received an request from the Department of the Secretary of State for thirty-two AES word processors. The order, however, offended a conscientious government purchasing officer who felt that it was unfair and perhaps wasteful of public money to buy the machines without inviting bids from competing suppliers. The official called Dorsey to learn whether he would be able to bid for the order and, if he were to win, deliver the machines on time. "The difficulty was that this was the beginning of March and the government's financial year closed at the end of the month," Dorsey recounts. "We were already working on orders for thirty-five machines, which was way above our production capacity. But, being young and entrepreneurial, we said we would like to bid. AES thought they were shoo-ins, so they didn't touch their price."

Micom normally charged about 10 per cent more than AES, but for this contract Dorsey dropped his price to 20 per cent below AES's. Although Micom won the order, the purchase order was delayed until March 17. This meant that Micom would have to produce five times its normal monthly output in less than two weeks. "This poor fellow in the government asked, 'Steve, can you do it?'

"I said, 'Don't worry.' Then I started to worry. We didn't have all the parts and we didn't have the printers. I phoned our printer supplier in California and they said delivery would take ninety days."

The printers were crucial to Micom's ability to deliver the government order, and Dorsey was determined to get the thirty-two that he needed, even though he had never been able to pay the printer manufacturer in advance for previous shipments. The California company was understandably reluctant to send that many of the three-thousand-dollar machines to a Canadian company that wanted them on credit. "One of the rules of low-budget financing," says Dorsey, "is never to show suppliers a statement, because they'll stop supplying. We never showed financial statements to anybody because we knew it couldn't help, it could only hurt." Micom had already exhausted its fifty-thousand-dollar line of credit at Dorsey's new bank, the Bank of Nova Scotia, and Dorsey approached Canadian Financial Company, whose usual business was lending to clothing manufacturers on the strength of payments owed to them. Canadian Financial, a subsidiary of the Bank of Virginia, had already learned something about the word-processing industry from negotiations with Innocan, which had wanted it to finance leasing arrangements for AES machines. But when Innocan suddenly struck a deal with a competitor, Canadian Financial felt that the investment company had reneged on an agreement. Canadian Financial, says Dorsey, "had its own axe to grind with AES." The financing firm advanced Dorsey the $100,000 he needed to buy the printers from California. Canadian Financial eventually would swell its stake in Micom to $1.5 million, and Dorsey says that confidence was the cause of Micom's ultimate success. Money in hand, he called the California printer maker and offered to pay cash if delivery could be made immediately. The printers were on their way to Micom within hours. Though he has no proof of this, Dorsey likes to think they were diverted from a shipment meant for AES.

Dorsey found a local metal worker who quickly made the metal chassis for the machines, but Micom's ability to assemble and test the internal circuit boards was severely strained. "Everybody, including me, started to assemble boards. My biggest concern was that we give the government value," he says. "We couldn't ship empty boxes or do anything fraudulent. What we did was just put the units together with absolutely no time to test them. We worked right up to five in the morning on March 31."

The untested word processors were loaded into a rented truck for a pre-dawn drive to Ottawa. "Our biggest fear was that the elevator would fail," says Dorsey. "If it had, we would never have made it." Each machine had to be delivered to a different location, and the last was unloaded at 11:30 p.m., thirty minutes before the federal fiscal year expired. Unfortunately, only seven of the machines had been tested.

Dorsey convinced the Secretary of State department that the machines should enter service in stages as operators were properly trained to run them. In the meantime, Micom was assembling duplicate sets of circuit boards, testing them, and then exchanging them for the hastily assembled and faulty boards as it brought each government machine into service at a rate of four a week.

In the end, says Dorsey, everyone was happy, except of course the rival that had lost the bid. "AES was furious. They went absolutely crazy and went to all levels in the government to try to block this order. Afterwards they accused us of shipping empty boxes."

In the United States, another big break came when the National Aeronautics and Space Administration ordered twenty-two of the word processors built in an attic on rue Ste-Hélène for use at NASA's space centre at Cape Canaveral. By the end of 1977, Micom had delivered about 350 machines in Canada and the United States and faced the problem of financing rapid growth. By then, fortunately for the company, the worth of word processing and office computer systems was understood by big investors, including Northern Telecom, which had rebuffed Dorsey's attempt to interest it in a share of AES.

But now Dorsey could afford to be choosy in his choice of a partner, and he was determined to avoid the sort of personality conflicts that had poisoned his sale of AES to Innocan. It was the tough personality of Northern's president, John Lobb, that caused him to repel Northern's advances, Dorsey says. "I thought that he was good for Northern but that he wouldn't be good for me. He's ruthless. I'd had enough of that. I wanted to enjoy business. I admire what he did for Northern, but I didn't want to be part of it."

Dorsey did, however, like another set of suitors, the Netherlanders who ran the Canadian operations of the Dutch multinational Philips NV. Philips was already selling a basic word processor made in Europe and discovered that the technological leader in North America was Micom. The Philips executives rode the cranky elevator to Dorsey's modest attic workshop and proposed a deal. Dorsey was wary because of his bad experience with AES. "I was concerned about getting involved with a multinational. One of the reasons people start companies is that they don't feel particularly comfortable in a big corporate environment." But he was attracted by what he calls the "culture" of Philips, which includes a faith in decentralized decision making. Philips proposed a deal by which part of what Dorsey was paid would be related to Micom's performance as a Philips subsidiary. The arrangement would guarantee Micom a great deal of autonomy for what was then still a small, attic operation. The Philips men who proposed the deal jested that if their management board back in Holland were ever to see what they were buying they would all be fired.

Dorsey was invited to Holland to meet the home office bosses. "It's overwhelming when you're still a little guy," Dorsey says. "They sent me first-class tickets and had a Mercedes waiting to take me to the hotel in Eindhoven owned by Philips for its visiting employees. It is like it must have been in the old Roman days with the legionaries coming in from the provinces." Negotiations lasted eight months before conclusion of an agreement that gave Philips 80-per-cent ownership of Micom with an option to buy Dorsey's remaining 20 per cent after five years. During that five years, Philips and Dorsey would share equally in Micom profits and Dorsey would continue as president. In May 1983, Philips exercised the option to take full ownership of Micom and at the same time renewed Dorsey's mandate as president for another two years. Dorsey won't reveal the full amount he was paid by Philips but concedes that it was "comfortable."

"After I made the deal with Philips I realized what pressure I'd been under my whole life," Dorsey sighs. "All of a sudden the house wasn't at risk as it had been pretty well throughout my business career. Suddenly I found myself in a situation where nothing was at risk. The worst thing that could happen was that things wouldn't get better."

With the money and the world-wide marketing network of Philips behind it, the Micom plant moved from its attic in Old Montreal back to the industrial zone where Dorsey had started out. This time, however, it was to a new modern plant not far from the AES factory. Philips backing also meant Micom's staff increased from thirty to a workforce of fifteen hundred in Canada and the United States. Monthly sales average about $20 million. Another number Dorsey takes some delight in is Micom's sales position as number three among major word processor manufacturers, behind IBM and Wang- -but one rank ahead of AES.

Since 1978, control of the profitable AES has been held directly by Canada Development Corporation. The US firm Lanier Products has 22 per cent of AES's shares and distributes its Montreal-made machines in the United States. Both companies are running fast in the research and development race essential to improve their positions as promoters of the electronic office and, although he has handed over ownership of Micom to a multinational, Dorsey says he still feels like an entrepreneur. Today, as far as Dorsey is concerned, the two companies born of his late-blooming ambition have settled into normal competition. "Nobody I hated is left at AES," he says. "The whole vendetta aspect has faded."

CHAPTER FIVE

A Clash of Symbols

The lobby of I.P. Sharp's international headquarters on the nineteenth floor of the Exchange Tower in Toronto is dominated by a mural map of the world whose countries are tied by glowing lights and a web of coloured lines reaching from Zurich to Singapore, from Helsinki to Dallas. The lines trace I.P. Sharp Associates' own global communications network. From five hundred cities in thirty-five countries, a local telephone call will connect Sharp's clients directly with the eighteenth-floor computer centre. At any one time, up to three hundred separate users may be plugged into the main computer from points on opposite sides of the earth. I.P. Sharp pays $250,000 a month to lease the lines of its international network. The computer and cables make up the factory of I.P. Sharp Associates, prototypal enterprise of the age of information, with revenues of $1 million a week from selling an invisible product.

One I.P. Sharp customer is the world's biggest producer of business forms, Moore Corporation of Toronto, which uses the network to collect financial information from its foreign offices. International airlines retrieve aviation information from some of the one hundred I.P. Sharp data bases. For annual fees as high as $32,000, plus the average hourly $300 levied for its use, international oil dealers employ the I.P. Sharp system to trade shiploads of crude by bargaining through direct, confidential messages between their terminals. Now Sharp has opened the system to smaller users and provides a communications program to turn IBM Personal Computers into Sharp terminals that can connect with the Toronto computer through the telephone line.

Sharp's computer runs on Universal time, and the system is at its busiest at mid-morning in Toronto when the tidal bore of North America's business day encounters the afternoon climax of business activity in Europe. Sharp's strategy is to prolong its computer's own business day by expanding into the Far East, where users would tap into the Toronto computer after Europe and America had gone to bed. Sharp's Hong Kong office has just translated its name into a Chinese expression of three characters whose pronunciation is similar to I.P. Sharp but which, individually, mean *elegant*, *wide spectrum*, and *in depth*. Together the characters signify a well-informed person. Twenty years afterward, McLuhan's once obscure declarations are revealed in their wisdom. "Just as light is at once energy and information," he wrote in *Understanding Media*, "so electric automation unites production, consumption and learning." Nowhere is McLuhan's analysis of automation more evident than in I.P. Sharp Associates, whose founding president, Ian Sharp, has reduced the definition of his business to a simple "We sell electrons."

The hallways of I.P. Sharp's three floors are painted in sensuous mauve and grey, and the walls are hung with a permanent exhibition of photographs made by members of I.P. Sharp's international staff. But the mellow ambience cools between the office area and the two-thirds of the eighteenth floor that is occupied by I.P. Sharp's computer centre. This sanctum stays permanently locked, and entry can be gained only by permission requested through the phone set hanging by the glass door.

The computer centre is dominated by a long, glass-enclosed "bridge," which does in fact resemble very much the bridge of a modern ship. Fourteen keyboard terminals allow the operators to monitor and control the three big computers they can see through the safety glass. The large machines are delicate and maintained by life support systems that ensure their survival in just the right atmosphere of clean, cool, and humid air, with guaranteed supplies of electricity and refreshing water to carry away the heat that the power generates as it courses through their circuitry. The bridge is manned every moment of the year by human and electronic lookouts. On the rear wall, a large grey panel maps the location of the 240 smoke detectors implanted in the ceilings and underneath the floors where the cables run. Another device monitors the flow of cooling water from tanks mounted on the rooftop of the Exchange Tower. In the basement is I.P. Sharp's own diesel-powered electricity plant, which automatically cuts into operation whenever Ontario Hydro's lines fail.

Outside the bridge, on the floor with the machines themselves, the air is as chill and damp as in a meat locker. One branch of the L-shaped machine room is occupied by the main control system of the company's private packet switching network. The opposite branch looks like a laundromat for an army. Twelve long rows of squat machines that resemble clothes washers contain the 40 billion characters of information available in an instant to I.P. Sharp customers. At the joint of the L, the main computer, a blue, $5.5-million IBM 3081, rests like the sarcophagus of a giant, motionless but intimidating.

Back up on the nineteenth floor, there is none of the bustle between rooms that might be expected of an international headquarters of a company whose six hundred employees are at work in fifty branches across the world. Here unending agendas of meetings are not part of the executive ritual, and paper memos are simply banned. Telephones do not ring. During the nearly three hours of the one workday morning when Sharp recounted the story of his company, his telephone set didn't interrupt once. And not because his secretary was intercepting his calls. There are no secretaries at I.P. Sharp, not even for Ian Sharp.

All internal messages travel by electronic mail, typed by the sender at a terminal, no matter where in the world he or she may be, and dispatched over I.P. Sharp's international network to its Toronto nerve centre, where the computer sorts incoming messages and waits for the addressee to request his mail. The locations of the sender and receiver are absolutely irrelevant. It sometimes happens that each believes the other to be at home in their headquarters offices when in fact one may be in Hong Kong and the other in Oslo. Occasionally, the place of origin is more obvious, as in a message sent to Ian Sharp's terminal from his marketing services manager, Rosanne Wild. It read:

FROM RWI TO IPS

GREETINGS...KONICHIWA...FROM JAPAN. NOTHING I COULD HAVE READ WOULD HAVE PREPARED ME FOR THIS COUNTRY! I EXPECTED MORE

PEOPLE TO SPEAK ENGLISH, BUT THAT IS NOT THE CASE AT ALL.

FOR INSTANCE, MOST OF THE EMPLOYEES AT THE HOTEL DON'T HAVE A CLUE IN HELL WHAT'S GOING ON IN ENGLISH SO YOU HAVE TO GET PEOPLE TO WRITE DOWN IN JAPANESE EVERYTHING YOU WANT TO KNOW AND SHOW IT TO THEM.

I AM AWAITING MR. TAMOIRI TO TALK ABOUT GLOBAL LIMITS, MICRO-COM, EMIS, ETC. HE'S QUITE FUNNY! AND VERY NICE. I BROUGHT HIM A SMALL GIFT AS WELL AS A BOTTLE OF SCOTCH WHICH HE MUCH APPRECIATED.

SAYONARA...ROSANNE.

Ian Sharp is the kind of man who makes the Irish believe in leprechauns. Impish, and wary, Sharp doesn't open up before the persistence and purpose of his questioner have been tested with a frustrating series of long pauses and short answers. And when he does, it can be with a fist-thumping fury or a spontaneous flash of a smile. Perhaps a more placid personality would have been unable to keep one foot firmly planted in the future.

Sharp was born in Dublin in 1932, but his family left Ireland for England when he was only a few weeks old. Sharp never settled anywhere or in any one school for very long. When he finished his studies in mechanical engineering at Cambridge, he did not apply for entry to the engineering orders, which, like lawyers' bar associations, control access to the profession. "I never bothered to do anything about it," explains Sharp, for whom bureaucracy of any kind (and perhaps even the mere physical presence of paper) seems to be an intolerable irritant.

Sharp's first experience with computers was in the English steel centre of Sheffield, where in 1958 he worked on the debugging of a computer program set up to simulate the performance of a new steel plant then being designed by United Steel Companies. Sharp had had no training as a programmer. He says, "I've never taken a programming course in my life. You get the manual and you read it. It doesn't take very long to learn how to write programs, particularly when you have a specific problem you're addressing. Lack of computer expertise doesn't matter very much."

Sharp left England for Canada in 1960 and adamantly refuses to attach any significance to either his decision to leave or his choice of a new country. "No particular reason. I was footloose and fancy free.

108

Canada didn't represent the land of opportunity or anything like that." Perhaps Sharp just doesn't want to give satisfaction to Canadians wallowing in what he considers to be narrow parochialism.

The Defence Research Board offered Sharp a job in Ottawa, but as it required security clearance Sharp had to wait for the RCMP to investigate his background. "After a couple of weeks of sitting around doing nothing, I got a bus to Toronto," the impatient Sharp says. There he found work as a programmer with Ferranti-Packard Limited, the Canadian subsidiary of the British firm that made the computer Sharp used in Sheffield. Ferranti's Canadian operation was just then building an entirely Canadian computer, the FP6000. It would be the first time-sharing computer that could handle the tasks of several users simultaneously. Perhaps ominously, the machine was being built in the airport building that a few years earlier had housed A.V. Roe Canada, whose technically successful Avro Arrow fighter plane, and much of Canadian aerospace expertise, was killed by the Conservative government of the late John Diefenbaker.

Sharp rose quickly to become chief programmer of the FP6000 project, and he hired a team of people to write the basic software for the new computer. The hardware engineers worked with the machine during the day. Sharp's software designers took over when the engineers went home – "We worked through the night until morning, at least twelve hours a day and weekends. There was no clocking in or anything like that."

Sharp's romantic interest was sparked by Audrey Williams, one of the programmers he had recruited, and in 1963, they interrupted their absorbing schedule to be married. Sharp says, "We didn't work that weekend."

The FP6000 was a success, and seven machines had been delivered by 1964 when the British government decided that its computer industry should be consolidated under one company, International Computers and Tabulators, commonly known as ICT. Ferranti's computer division was sold to ICT, and the design of the Canadian FP6000 went to England. Several thousand of the computers were made in Britain; in fact, the machine became ICT's main product during the next ten years.

In Canada, however, Ferranti's fifty hardware engineers and software designers were out of work. At the same time, Canadian capacity to build major computers was annihilated, and attempts by the team to promote another project met with national apathy. Ferranti-Packard had not even been able to sell its Canadian-made machine to Canadian governments. "There was a total lack of support for that development from the government at all levels. There was no interest in Canada at that time in preserving that expertise," Sharp says. "There was a general attitude that if a computer was made here it couldn't possibly be as good as one that was made somewhere else."

Did this surprise the then recent immigrant? He says it still does. "On the whole, Canadians don't tend to think in global terms. They think parochially."

Before they were officially laid off, Sharp and seven of his programmers quit to set up their own company. Ferranti, with great relief, passed on to them the job of providing service to the existing customers of its now defunct computer division. The fledgling entrepreneurs scraped together $4,300 to provide the start-up capital for I.P. Sharp Associates.

Sharp now recalls, "We took office space in the basement of a building at Lawrence and Keele. If I remember rightly, it was two hundred a month, but we got the first two months rent free in exchange for decorating the place ourselves. We all showed up on a Saturday morning and painted it." The eight were unequal partners, but the percentage of ownership was not determined by how much of the $4,300 each partner had contributed. "It was done in terms of my arbitrary assessment of the value of the people," Sharp says. His 18 per cent was the biggest share. Audrey Sharp was not among the founding partners in December 1964. She was pregnant with the first of the couple's two children; later she would work intermittently for the company as she raised them.

The first customer for the new company's computer programs was the Toronto Stock Exchange. "We had a reasonably good reputation as a software development group within the industry at the time the company was set up," Sharp remembers. One of the new firm's major assets was Roger Moore, a founding partner and vice-president who already had a personal reputation for programming genius in the industry. "So we in fact didn't have a great deal of trouble in getting business. It took us, I think, about three months to become operationally profitable. We didn't go into debt, but on the other hand we didn't pay ourselves for the first three months. After six or nine months we had paid off our back salaries and we were operating profitably and generating cash. I think I was making $10,000 a year as president. The lowest salary, I think, was $6,000."

In 1966, I.P. Sharp Associates received a contract from no less distinguished an institution than the IBM Research Center at Yorktown Heights, N.Y. IBM wanted Roger Moore to work at Yorktown Heights with a Canadian-born mathematician named Kenneth Iverson who was transferring APL, a programming language he had invented, from theory to reality as a computer time-sharing system. The brilliant, dishevelled Moore was to spend a year on that project. He returned an APL enthusiast. In 1969, after moving up in the world to the forty-second floor of the downtown TD Centre, I.P. Sharp Associates installed their first leased computer with the intention of starting a commercial time-sharing service based on APL.

The company needed a million dollars to finance the time-sharing service, and Sharp went to an investment brokerage firm with his plan. For their commission of about $25,000 the brokers brought potential investors and Sharp together in their offices. "We couldn't promise anything," recalls Sharp. "APL was then an unknown language but was obviously productive in terms of program development time. You could develop an application much quicker than in any of the conventional programming languages. We thought that enough people would realize this and that we could sell a service."

The quest for investors lasted several months as the brokers set up meeting after meeting at which Sharp would present his scheme. In his description, "We'd spend the whole morning talking to them about what it was we were planning to do. Some of them didn't like the idea, so they went away, and some of them did. Eventually it was something like six investors who put up the money." One of the select group was the Dofasco pension fund and another was Charterhouse, the British investment company. The partners gave up 20 per cent of their company for the million dollars, and since then the number of shareholders has grown to about three hundred. But I.P. Sharp Associates remains a private company in which only employees may hold voting shares, and Ian Sharp still controls 12 per cent of it all.

The time-sharing business did not prosper as quickly as Sharp had expected. The company lost about half a million dollars in the first two years. But by 1971, APL time sharing had caught on, and the company's growth zoomed by an average compound rate of 35 per cent each year, thanks to the invention dreamed up by a prairie farm boy whose initial schooling stopped when he was thirteen.

Distinguished by strong, handsome facial features below a mane of thick salt-and-pepper hair, Kenneth Iverson retains the country boy's confiding, open regard, honest blue eyes, and strong handshake. His direct, unpretentious manner owes more to his youth on the Canadian prairie than to his adult career amid the ivy of Boston. His speech is simple and clear, without academic ums, ahs, or hesitations.

Iverson was born in 1920 to a family that had come from South Dakota seventeen years earlier to homestead at Camrose, Alberta. "When I say Camrose that's actually just putting on the dog, because actually we were twenty miles from Camrose, which was the nearest town," Iverson laughs. He was well into adulthood before he knew that there was such a thing as higher education. It was by fluke of war that he returned to school, taught at Harvard, invented APL, and came to be honoured as a great master of computing. In 1979, the computer world's highest award, the A.M. Turing prize, named for the British scientist who used secret computers to break enemy military codes during the Second World War, was given to Iverson for his invention.

A programming language is a sort of bionic equivalent of Esperanto, synthesized from elements of human thought and unforgiving mechanical logic. It is the means by which man communicates his desires to the machine. All computer software, the programs that decide whether a machine will be, for the moment, a word processor or a complex calculator, a communications terminal or a toy, are written in one or another of the dozens of programming languages developed in the past twenty years.

Programming languages such as BASIC, FORTRAN, and COBOL bear a superficial resemblance to each other because of their use of ungainly but often comprehensible words like GOTO, PRINT, and INKEY$. Like religions, programming languages attract convinced followers who have been converted to their complex lexicons and arcane logics. Nevertheless, most programming languages are essentially alike though, like Baptists and Catholics, their followers perceive the differences more than the similarities.

112

APL is one programming language that *is* fundamentally different. From its hub in Toronto, it is reaching out to an international élite of thousands of economic and financial analysts. APL, with an honesty rare among acronyms, means simply "A Programming Language." It is not the easiest language to learn, but it is probably the best for analysing numbers, whether they are for international oil production statistics or for the consolidated accounts of a big multinational corporation. APL was designed to deal with graphs and tables of numbers and can flip them around, pile them on top of each other, and extract useful information from them in ways that would be tedious or impossible with other programming languages.

APL was used to animate sequences of the Disney movie *TRON*. It is an exceptionally graphic language, both in its use of symbols instead of truncated words to express actions and in its ability to deal in direction and dimension. Its characters are inspired not only by English but by Greek and to some extent by pictographic symbols. APL is above all a language of symbols, which often evoke their meaning visually. Arrows, stars, and dominoes are used where other languages would employ words or phrases, or couldn't accomplish the task at all. If the table

$$A \quad B \quad C$$
$$D \quad E \quad F$$
$$G \quad H \quad I$$

is to be flipped diagonally so that it becomes

$$A \quad D \quad G$$
$$B \quad E \quad H$$
$$C \quad F \quad I$$

The APL instruction is:

$$\phi$$

An entire line of an APL program can look like this:

$$CONTOURMAP\Diamond \quad ' \quad .\circ O \star \circledast '[+/[1]\alpha \circ .\leq \omega]$$

The originality of APL is in its three-dimensional definition of sets of numbers and its use of graphic symbols to represent mathematical

113

manipulation of those sets of numbers. "To anybody who thinks graphically or pictorially there is no complication," says Iverson. "Other languages simply have never seriously addressed the question of using tables or graphic symbols. We have assumed the freedom to design our own character set, which means we can use graphic symbols. In particular we did what the Chinese did by recognizing that you can make more complicated signs by superimposing others. The very symbolism suggests things to you."

Iverson calls some of APL's symbols "visual puns." For example, the use of a circle enclosing a star, which resembles the cross section of a tree trunk, means *logarithm*. APL's total lack of English words makes it a truly universal language that can be understood equally well by users from any country and even by blind programmers, who use a Braille version. Although it was not his intention, Iverson has in fact achieved some of the original aim of Melville Bell, whose own life work was the invention of a universal alphabet that could be understood by anyone and particularly the deaf. The telephone, at least according to McLuhan, was a by-product of the Bells' quest for a mechanical means of rendering human speech in a visible language the way Braille turns visible language into tactile language.

APL could not, of course, have been implemented using the ordinary typewriter keyboard common with computer terminals. But IBM's introduction of the Selectric replaceable typing element in 1961 meant that only the ball would have to be changed, not the entire terminal. "The Selectric came along at the right time when we were doing the implementation, and we realized that we could actually design our character set and typeface," Iverson recalls. By creating a unique APL symbolism, Iverson and his collaborators could simplify the expression of programming ideas. "You can have badly written APL that's almost impossible to decipher just as you can have badly written English, or badly written FORTRAN. But the fact that you can condense something that might take ten pages in FORTRAN into half a dozen lines of APL means that you have some hope," he says.

More than 100,000 copies of APL instruction books have been sold, and there are thousands of special APL terminals plugged into big time-sharing computer centres in Canada and in the United States. APL has become the common programming language of computing's Brahman caste.

114

Kenneth Iverson now does his thinking from an office in I.P. Sharp Associates' international headquarters. Within jumping distance of his desk is his blackboard, scribbled full with red, green, yellow, and white chalk. In one upper corner is Iverson's agenda for the day. The rest is overrun with a jumble of symbols, numbers, and delicious phrases like "numerical precision" and "honest math." From his office he has a clear view of the railway yards behind Union Station and the roundhouse, water tower, and coal chutes erected to service the last, beautiful behemoths of the steam age. Behind Iverson's swivel chair, just as black as the locomotives that once smudged the air behind Front Street, is a terminal linked to I.P. Sharp's 3081, the biggest machine IBM has yet made to power the age of information.

It was during the Depression that Iverson quit school after finishing Grade Ten. He became a farm worker and might have remained one all his life if he hadn't joined the Royal Canadian Air Force in 1943 with an ambition to become a pilot. "I was for the first time thrown in with people who had some education. Before that I hadn't the foggiest idea about the existence of universities or professions." While training to become not the pilot he wanted to be but a flight engineer, Iverson caught up on his high school education through correspondence courses provided by the Canadian Legion. Iverson made it only as far as Newfoundland before the war in Europe ended, and after being released from the service and determined to continue his learning, he went to Ottawa to study at the new Carleton College which helped many veterans catch up on their education. He was twenty-six years old and had been out of school for a dozen years.

It is to his late academic start that Iverson attributes his success. "It's probably bias on my part, but I tend to find over and over that the interesting people and ones who in my estimation do interesting things usually have unusual educational backgrounds." After Carleton, Iverson was admitted to the mathematics department at Queen's University where he won the Prince of Wales medal for the best overall four-year record.

He was offered a four-hundred-dollar scholarship by Harvard University – hardly enough to buy necessary books – but the Canadian government's veterans' program, which Iverson praises as "very enlightened," continued to support him in Boston. "I had heard and read a little bit about computers, which at the time were just coming into being, and realized after I got to Harvard that this was the centre of activities, that this was where Professor Aiken had built his Mark I computer. He went on to build four computers in all, and I quickly got interested in that."

Howard Aiken was Iverson's mentor, and although he died in 1970, Iverson hardly ever lets ten minutes go by without quoting Aiken or praising his wisdom. With $500,000 in parts, engineering help and factory assembly donated by IBM, Aiken completed his Mark I computer in 1944. It was the first modern computer and functioned for fifteen years. "By the time other universities were beginning to get really interested in building computers, Aiken said that the time for universities to be building computers was passed," Iverson relates. "The manufacturers were recognizing computers as something that would pay. He said it was time for the universities to turn their attention to some other things. One was applications and the other was education. At the time I was about to graduate, Aiken was busily organizing a program he called data processing. So I stayed there and taught for six years in a graduate program which was the precursor of computer science."

Iverson had another guide at Harvard besides Aiken. His second thesis adviser was the Nobel Prize economist Wassily Leontief, whom Aiken had invited to explore the uses computers might have for his analyses. Iverson became a matchmaker in the union of data processing and economic analysis and wrote a doctoral thesis entitled "Applications of a Dynamic Economic Model."

This 1954 thesis already included a simple language for the handling of matrix algebra. "I was exploring ways of solving Leontief's problems which arose in economics and I realized fairly early that if I had to really reprogram from scratch in machine language every area that I wanted to explore, I would be there forever," Iverson explains. "When I first started, the only languages were machine languages. The computer I worked on most at Harvard was Aiken's last machine, the Mark IV. If you wanted to add two numbers you'd have to say 'Load 80,' meaning 'Load from register 80,' and then you'd say, 'Add register 81,' and then, 'Store register 82.' You'd have to break it down into a sequence like that, but in fact you wouldn't say 'load,' 'store,' and so on – there were codes for those. One would be 01, one would be 02, one would be 03. You simply had to learn those codes."

116

Iverson invented his own set of notations for expressing mathematical operations that would accomplish the manipulations required by Leontief's theories, but "it wasn't called APL. It wasn't called anything." And it wasn't, during his Harvard career, ever implemented on a computer. It remained a theoretical language which he used with his students to describe mathematical operations. "I always had it in the back of my mind that, yes, this thing should be implemented on a computer and in fact was always rather disappointed that nobody was really interested in doing such a thing."

Iverson left Harvard in 1960, not because he was unhappy there but because he didn't get tenure and therefore, by Harvard tradition, was expected to leave. He had close friends working at IBM and was attracted by IBM's new research centre at Yorktown Heights which, almost without question, gave its staff freedom to explore. "It was at that time, I'd say, very loose in that they were looking for people with ideas." In fact, he was told by a staff member, "If you have a reasonable-sounding idea and really want to work on it, management will buy it because they're at their wit's end to know what to do." What Iverson wanted to do was simply to continue work on formalizing his new language and writing his first book about it. IBM took him on, and more than doubled his pay as a Harvard professor.

Iverson stayed with the computer giant until 1980, working at turning his set of original mathematical symbols into a useful computer language. By his account, the system was running and being used within IBM in the fall of 1966. "Back in those days, the issue of software was much looser. In fact IBM did not market software at all. Software was simply something they developed and provided in order to market their machines. So there was no extra charge for it." There was never a copyright or patent to protect APL, and Iverson didn't want one. "Professor Aiken advised us all very strongly not to get involved in patents. One of his sayings that I still treasure was, 'Don't worry about anybody stealing your ideas. If they're original, you'll have to ram them down their throats.'"

IBM never satisfied Iverson that its salesmen were promoting APL as an alternative to the older, linear languages. It was certainly not getting as much attention from IBM as it was enjoying at I.P. Sharp Associates. The Toronto company had started its time-sharing service using a version of APL supplied by IBM, which by 1970 was leasing rather than giving away its computer software. But as their APL business picked up, I.P. Sharp's programmers kept expanding and modifying the IBM software until they had revised it so much that it bore little resemblance to the original IBM version. I.P. Sharp then informed IBM that it was no longer using the IBM software and stopped paying the licence fee.

Iverson's Canadian-born son Eric, a blue-jeaned Yale dropout with a droopy blond moustache, was, when his father left IBM, in charge of the thirty-five I.P. Sharp programmers who are constantly at work in Toronto, Rochester, Palo Alto, and Amsterdam improving APL. Five of Iverson's colleagues in the development of APL at IBM had also gone to the Toronto company. It was obvious by 1980 that I.P. Sharp was doing more than IBM in the evolution of APL, and Iverson decided that it was the place for him too. "I simply felt that the way things were going, I would have much more influence with what happened with APL here than I would have any place else. This was the one company that was really totally devoted to APL."

Iverson believes that learning a programming language, in other words learning to communicate with a machine, changes the thinking of the human brain. "I'm confident it does, but in the same sense that learning English and learning to write changes your way of thinking. Language really is a tool of thought. You can't think complicated thoughts without thinking in some language. Furthermore, it's an exceedingly important change, the importance being the discipline: the fact that the rules are simple and rigorous."

But anger rises in his voice when he speaks of the mystical significance attached to the act of programming by many professors of computer science and the promoters of other computer languages. "I recently spent about twenty hours on a plane with the head of a computer science department, and he told me, 'We're really teaching something new – we're teaching problem solving.' I think that's absolutely dangerous nonsense, and computer scientists are influential enough so that it will probably affect our teaching. I think it's going to be an absolute disaster. However, it will be pronounced a success, because how do you measure the results?"

Perhaps the most spectacular success built upon making a mystique of the programming process belongs to a Montreal company that has made a commercial product of another language developed in Boston. Logo Computer Systems was formed in 1980 to market the language called LOGO. The wildfire propagation of LOGO and the catechism that goes with it provide a revealing contrast with the penetration of APL, which has been long and incomplete. LOGO is as simple as APL is difficult and has been imbued by its promoters with powers reminiscent of those of the cloth of silk and gold visible only to wise men in Hans Christian Andersen's tale, "The Emperor's New Clothes." Unlike Iverson, who debunks notions of programming as a higher calling, LOGO's promoters attach spiritual significance to the act of guiding a so-called "turtle" about the screen.

LOGO emerged in the 1970s from the Artificial Intelligence Laboratory of Massachusetts Institute of Technology when Iverson's APL was already running on IBM computers at I.P. Sharp Associates. Essentially, LOGO is a set of instructions, entered from the keyboard, that controls the movements of a pointer, or turtle, which, like a skywriting airplane, can trace patterns or simple sketches on the screen. One of LOGO's big selling points is that it can be learned by preschoolers. To LOGO's proselytizers, the process of making a LOGO program teaches children the procedure of "debugging." If the turtle scampers off the wrong way, the child can change the faulty instruction instantly and see the results on the screen. This immediate feedback is the source of LOGO's reputed power to improve the mind.

LOGO's inventor is Seymour Papert, a professor of mathematics and education who attracted among his academic disciples a Montrealer named Guy Montpetit, a charming scholastic vagabond in his mid-forties. Montpetit became a devotee of LOGO, and when the wave of personal computers began to break over North America at the beginning of the 1980s, Montpetit decided that the time was ripe to make a commercial product of it. To accomplish the deed, he attracted into his company a salesman par excellence named Jean Baroux, who was born in Casablanca in 1946 and immigrated to Ottawa with his parents when Morocco became independent.

Baroux did for LOGO in months what other people's years of dogged effort have been unable to do for APL – endow it with a kind of religious legitimacy among educators and computer salesmen. According to Baroux, "A child sitting at a computer with LOGO is a child free to explore with the most powerful tool mankind has ever been able to develop. It's not an environment of right and wrong, it's the debugging of ideas."

He explains his methods: "We spent a great deal of time on the phone with writers and editors of magazines and newspapers to convince them that we had the greatest thing since sliced bread. So eventually you get through to a few people and they start looking at it seriously. Then an article got published, and then a second and it snowballed to the point where we had thousands of articles written about LOGO."

As the media blitz picked up frenzy, Baroux commuted to California in a door-to-door canvass of computer makers. He wanted an endorsement of LOGO by a well-known manufacturer whose credibility would give the software instant legitimacy. In October 1981, Logo completed a crucial and unique contract with Apple Computer of California. For the first time, Apple agreed to co-label a product with an outside supplier. It was also the first time it had signed a contract with a supplier outside the United States. LOGO was still far from ready when that contract was signed. "They believed us and we delivered, but we didn't have a product when we signed the contract," Baroux says.

LOGO finally hit the stores in March 1982, supported by an Apple advertising campaign in computer and educational magazines. Baroux flips through the pages of *Byte* to find the LOGO ad: "It's got Apple's name on it. It looks like an Apple ad. It's the first time Apple has ever dedicated an ad to a piece of software." How did he get Apple to go so far in supporting another company's product? "I paid for it," he says, his voice dropping to a conspiratorial whisper. "I said, 'You develop the ad. We'll supply you with the copy and the pictures, and we'll pay for the placement.'"

Apple LOGO is recorded onto disks in a small plant not far from Logo's Montreal offices, sealed with the instruction book in a box labelled "Apple," and flown in air freight containers to Cupertino, California, Apple's distribution point. Even the packages sold in Montreal computer stores just a few blocks from the Logo offices have been to California and back.

Like APL and all other computer languages, LOGO is not protected by copyright, and anyone could have done with it what Baroux and Logo Computer Systems achieved by clever marketing. "I took a product that was in the public domain and made it ours by being there first, being there better, and signing everybody and his mother to a contract," boasts Baroux.

Iverson makes no secret of his disappointment that APL has so far failed to penetrate schools and a greater mass of small computer users, and I.P. Sharp Associates is now working on plans to produce versions of APL for personal computers. But LOGO's success is more an irritant than an inspiration to him. "The LOGO people talk about turtle geometry and so on as if they're inventing a great new geometry, and that's nonsense." He thinks the cultists of every computer language, including those of APL, can be compared with simple-minded evangelists who are sincere but shallow. "I don't think that the LOGO people are that dangerous because I don't think they are going to have all that much success. But that same attitude is having success in the university computer science departments, and that I find is much more frightening."

Despite Iverson's objections, even some I.P. Sharp employees demonstrate an almost LOGO-like commitment to Iverson's invention. Instructor Douglas Thompson of I.P. Sharp's Ottawa office, for example, wears an APL tie pin and drinks coffee from an APL mug. It has become a company axiom that the "linear thinking" of other computer languages "gives you brain damage," while Joey Tuttle, manager of I.P. Sharp's research centre at Palo Alto, affirms that good APL programmers are "right brained" because they can actually see the structure of an APL problem. Other programming languages "are definitely left brained (procedural, verbal, symbolic)," Tuttle argued in an electronic mail exchange between Bagsvaerd, Denmark, where he was travelling, and Hudson, Quebec, where this book was written.

As for Iverson, who technically works for his own son, he is now free to promote his language his own way by designing courses in APL and working to make it a common part of university computer curricula. His job description is simple: "Don't tell Ian, but I do what I want to do."

Ian Sharp claims never to have counted his customers. "It's a meaningless concept. Is a customer who has fifty terminals and spends $100,000 a month in the same league with a customer who signs on once a year and spends four cents? Does that mean you have two customers?" Aside from the APL time-sharing service, I.P. Sharp's computer also provides the world's most extensive electronic collection of financial and business data bases in what started out as a secondary activity but now gives the company its best complement to general time-sharing activity, which is tapering off as more and more users process their data on their own small computers. Electronic data bases can store and instantly retrieve quantities of information that no library could effectively manage if they were printed on paper. APL programs can then take the retrieved information and analyse it.

"We got into data bases in a very Mickey Mouse way," says Ian Sharp. "The first customers for time sharing were the brokers, and so the first data base that we developed was the Toronto Stock Exchange closing prices. We'd got seriously into data bases, I think, because in 1973 Air Canada had expressed an interest in aviation information. Air Canada didn't, in fact, become a customer, but word of what we were developing got to McDonnell Douglas and they got all fired up about it. It was really McDonnell Douglas pressure that got that data in and cleaned up." The aviation data originates with the Civil Aeronautics Board in Washington and is used by aircraft manufacturers like McDonnell Douglas and the world's airlines to follow industry trends. Banks that lend money to airlines and the aviation research departments of every big broker on Wall Street dip into the I.P. Sharp data, and more recently airport planners have become customers. Even the Civil Aeronautics Board, which gathers the information, uses I.P. Sharp's Toronto computer to retrieve it.

I.P. Sharp's financial data bases are the fastest growing of its library. They now include trading reports from all Canadian and American exchanges, the London Stock Exchange, the Sydney Stock Exchange, and most recently the Singapore and Hong Kong exchanges. Other information residing in I.P. Sharp memory banks includes monthly figures from the German Bundesbank, international economic forecasts, and a directory of equipment available to combat hazardous oil or chemical spills.

Sharp puts his electronic information operation in an entirely different class from electronic publishing directed at the home market, where consumers have become accustomed to having their information subsidized by advertising. "It's economically viable to plunk Telidon into people's houses and give it to them for free as long as you can get firms like the Dominion Stores of this world to pay for it. It's an ideal way of advertising. Eaton's could put up an electronic catalogue

122

which would save it an enormous amount of printing costs. But that's not data that I would regard as having intrinsic value."

The company continues its original business of selling software. Its fanciest product now is a program to control the manufacture of microchips. All six of the customers who paid the initial price of $200,000 and subsequent annual fees of $50,000 for the package are in California's Silicon Valley. Sharp estimates there are two thousand chip-manufacturing facilities in the United States. "The people who are making chips aren't necessarily those you would expect. Any company that's building any kind of sophisticated product has to be in the position of understanding at least the process of chip manufacturing. If, as an industry, you're dependent on somebody else to do your designing for you and somebody else to do your manufacturing, you're not leaving yourself very much."

Only Northern Telecom, Mitel, and Linear Technology make microchips in Canada, a fact Sharp attributes to the apathy and ignorance of Canada's traditional manufacturing industries. "People are not quite aware yet that this is the way the world is going. If somebody two years from now attempts to make a dishwasher that isn't computer controlled, he's not going to be able to sell it." Sharp concedes that, in the short run, some unemployment will ensue. "If a manufacturing industry does develop microelectronics technology, then certainly it will put a good chunk of its work force out of work. On the other hand, it will need to hire other sorts of people to operate the new systems. Furthermore, if it doesn't get into new technology, then it will lose 100 per cent of its work force because of competitive market pressures."

Sharp is an aggressive opponent of the protectionism that has dominated Canadian business and government philosophy. With the passing of the industrial age, taxes and tariffs are even more self-defeating as instruments of national economic health. "If you go back to these archaic ways of trying to protect these jobs," Sharp says, "we're all going to go out of business here. That sort of technique just doesn't work. It doesn't work in this business, and it doesn't work in the stove and refrigerator business. If we didn't have all these silly restrictions and taxes and tariffs, Ontario could be a haven for the information industry. Every hotel chain and airline has got to put in a computer system somewhere to run its reservation system, but the present rules of the game mean that under no circumstances would you dream of putting it in Canada. We're just losing opportunities. There could be literally thousands and thousands more jobs in the computer business in Toronto if the governments would create an environment which would encourage it."

Sharp calculates that his own company pays a penalty of $2 million a year to do business in Canada, all of it in federal and provincial tariffs and taxes. "Just look at IBM's prices. They're anywhere from 30 to 50 per cent higher here than in the United States, not including exchange." When you pay $5.5 million for a computer, as I.P. Sharp did for its main machine, 30 per cent counts. Sharp says that the company could eventually be forced to move out of Canada if the tax climate remains hostile. "Technically, it would be easy to relocate."

More than 70 per cent of Sharp's revenues come from outside Canada, a balance that he recognizes is not enjoyed by the Canadian data-processing industry as a whole. A few smaller Canadian companies, with some sympathy from Ottawa, want to spread the protectionist tariff tradition to data flowing across the border. The notion of taxing electrons at the border doubles Sharp's fury against excessive taxation and Canada's habitual recourse to protection of its home market for its own businesses. Instead of protecting its own, Canada should, to Sharp's mind, be going after the business of other countries. "Stop thinking so goddam parochially!" he shouts, with a firm thump of his fist on his desk. "It's a world market and we're losing our share of it."

After twenty years on the frontier of the information economy, Ian Sharp is still awed by his job as traffic cop to a global flow of electrons. His reflection seems no different from the first reaction of a visitor discovering with amazement that I.P. Sharp Associates has no tangible product. "It's frightening, isn't it?" reflects Ian Sharp.

CHAPTER SIX

The Light That Failed

Canadians claim significant pioneering successes in the distribution of information by computer. I.P. Sharp's international network is the most spectacular and most profitable, but two other companies have also become world leaders in the distribution of information from big computer libraries to computer screens in offices and homes.

Two Queen's University law professors, Hugh Lawford and Richard von Briesen saw, in 1973, the promise of a business in a pair of research projects they had directed. One was a compilation of treaties and agreements between countries formerly part of the British Empire. The other was a collaboration between Queen's and IBM Canada to see how computers could aid lawyers in their legal research. The two teachers incorporated QL Systems to purchase the results of those projects and set up a computerized library of Canadian law and jurisprudence that could be searched by lawyers wherever there was a telephone line. More privileged, or wiser, than most entrepreneurs, Lawford, the company president, maintained his professorship at Queen's while he built QL (for Quic Law) into a data base containing most federal and provincial laws and law reports. In the meantime, his team of programmers in Kingston was developing the most efficient aids to librarians since eyeglasses and hair buns. The Kingston group's software could search through masses of turgid legislation and court reports in seconds to retrieve material containing terms specified by the user sitting at his terminal in a law office hundreds or thousands of miles away, all for far less than it would cost to pay a legal librarian or junior lawyer to sift through the printed volumes that decorate the bookcases of law offices.

So successful was the searching software that QL's computer store expanded beyond the law to include the text of the daily Question Period in the House of Commons and indexes of writings about arctic technology, social life in the Yukon, the international coal industry, and other collections of esoteric or general interest information. QL also supplies the accumulated output of the Canadian Press news agency and is now encouraging the owners of personal computers to call the Kingston computers over the telephone system's Datapac network and retrieve information from QL's dozens of data bases.

QL's searching software has been sold to similar operations in Canada and the United States, including the Knight-Ridder newspaper chain, which uses QL software to provide a public computer library of stories published by the Philadelphia dailies, the *Inquirer* and the *Daily News*. The Kingston firm's software also powers Westlaw, the U.S. electronic library of case law, which operates on computers in St. Paul, Minnesota.

Canada's other online information pioneer is the *Globe and Mail* of Toronto. In 1977, when it abandoned making type from molten lead in favour of the new computerized systems, the *Globe* handed the computer tapes containing each edition over to QL Systems, whose computers created a public electronic library of the newspaper's stories. But the electronically clipped stories were running two or three weeks behind the paper's publication until 1979, when the *Globe* decided to accelerate the operation and make it a separate corporate division called Info Globe. The paper bought its search and retrieval software from QL Systems, modified it, and moved the electronic data base of earlier *Globe* stories from Kingston to Toronto, first to computers run by a time-sharing company called Datacrown and then to Canada Systems Group.

At the same time the *Globe*, with its daily rival the *Toronto Star* and with the Southam newspaper chain, was negotiating creation of a partnership between the three big newspaper companies. The *Globe* was to join in an electronic publishing venture called Infomart, which had been started by the *Star* and Southam in 1975 and was Canadian agent for a U.S. library of computer data bases that could be accessed by a computer terminal and a telephone call. The *Globe*'s electronic library would be Infomart's first Canadian product. The other two publishers were anxious to jump into the new technology of Telidon, which could transmit colour and graphics as well as text down the telephone lines. But the *Globe* soon decided that the commercial value of Telidon was dubious because it would require every data base user to have a special Telidon terminal. Its own Info Globe, on the other hand, worked with any communicating terminal, word processor, or personal computer. It pulled out of the proposed partnership, choosing instead to develop a market for Info Globe on its own. In January 1980, the paper hired Barbara Hyland to revitalize the service. Hyland is a formal, efficient woman who does, however, retain enough girlishness to refuse to state her age and to fold her legs under her as she curls into her office armchair for a chat. She was born in Sherbrooke, Quebec, and became a professional librarian. When the *Globe* asked her to take charge of Info Globe, she was working as sales manager of a small Toronto company called Micromedia, which produced indexes to Canadian business periodicals and other information on microfilm.

Hyland took home a small terminal and tried out the data base service she had been hired to run. She dialed the computer's number, connected the telephone to the terminal, and starting asking the computer for information. "It was magic, putting in a word and getting all those results back. It was terrific fun," she says. There were at the time only 120 paying subscribers to the Info Globe service, and even the paper's own reporters and editors rarely used it, finding it clumsy and not up to date.

Hyland applied some of the old romantic notions of newspaper publishing to the electronic technology, imposing the tyranny of the deadline on an operation that had originally lazed in the calm, quiet habits of the library. Each evening at nine o'clock, Info Globe's desk staff of two "enhancers" and one "indexer" arrive to process the content of the next day's newspaper for inclusion in its permanent data base. The day's stories are already in the paper's editorial computer and the job of the Info Globe workers is to add codes and titles so that they can be retrieved by the search software. At 3 a.m., the coded stories are copied from the computer onto a reel of magnetic tape and popped into a taxi for a twenty-three-dollar ride to the Canada Systems Group computer centre in Mississauga, where the average daily one million characters of information are immediately added to the Info Globe data base. The day's *Globe and Mail* is thus available in

127

homes in London or Paris or anywhere in North America hours before the company's orange trucks have delivered the paper to parts of Metropolitan Toronto. "We are unique in the world still in having moved the system from a library function to a part of the actual production of the newspaper," says Hyland. "It was in November 1980 that we were able to achieve what we call simultaneous publication, and I am very happy to say we have not missed a day yet." The accumulated Info Globe data base contains every story published in the *Globe* since January 1, 1978.

From a terminal in her office, Hyland can order the Canada Systems Group computers to reveal just who happens to be sifting through the *Globe's* electronic edition. One of the regular early morning browsers is Mobil Oil Corporation, which scans the paper from its U.S. headquarters. Occasionally, from Brussels, the multinational mining company Union Minière searches the data base. But the most exotic user, which dials into Info Globe from Washington, is identified on Hyland's screen as "The CIA."

The CIA or anyone else pays Info Globe $159 dollars for an hour of use, and that, Hyland believes, protects the traditional paper newspaper from the competition of its electronic sibling. "The fact is, for twenty-five cents you can get a million characters of information. I can't deliver that." Info Globe continues to stick with the technology of straight text transmission, without the colour and the graphics that Telidon videotex could provide. "We have stayed away from videotex. We didn't really feel that there is a market in the short term. We are certainly watching it."

Unfortunately for Telidon, a lot more people are watching the evolution of the whole videotex industry than are actually joining it, either as viewers or as suppliers of information. Five years after Telidon was unveiled by the federal communications department in 1978, the man who had then been director-general reponsible for the Telidon program is concerned that the propagation of Telidon technology is stalled. "Telidon is, I think, at a bit of a crisis point at the moment," says John Madden, now director of Microtel Pacific Research Centre in Burnaby. In Ottawa, as director of the Telidon program, Madden had been more than just the bureaucratic patron of the engineers doing the work in the Communications Research

Centre. He had argued, as most directors do, for more money to support his project but had used distinctly unbureaucratic means to get it. In his exhortations he defined the videotex technology as a national and social force for radical change. It was imperative, Madden suggested to other bureaucrats and to the politicians, that Canada be at the forefront of videotex technology to ensure that the country would benefit from it and have some influence over it.

Telidon is certainly still only a pale shadow of what Madden had imagined in his futurist descriptions of a world in which Telidon could be either a vast extension of the human brain or the Big Brother of Orwell's *1984*.

Madden is the author of "Julia's Dilemma," a chapter of *Gutenberg Two* in which a home communications system leads to such changes in social organization that, in the end, the world's population splits into two groups. There are the Humanity Firsters, who worry that the evolution of computer-controlled society is a threat to human biological survival, and the Brain Firsters, a smaller but wealthier and better-educated group of people who have unquestioning faith in electronics technology and artificial intelligence and who choose to exile themselves, with their machines, to Australia. In Madden's scenario, home computers had evolved into talking Alter Egos or AYEEs, as they had come to be called. "By the year 2000," a computer historian in "Julia's Dilemma" recounts, "the AYEEs had developed to the point where, by the purchase of a special attachment, widows were able to carry on conversations with their dead husbands' alter ego computers, although not with their actual husbands, who were indeed biologically dead."

John Madden was born in Vancouver in 1939. His father had emigrated to Canada from England at the age of eleven with his own father, who had been a poor clergyman in England and was enticed by the promise of a better life growing fruit in the Kootenay valley of British Columbia. The Kootenay orchards proved a disaster and the family moved to Victoria. Here the younger Madden, with the minimum of education, became first a self-taught marine engineer and then an aeronautical engineer during the Depression when the Boeing Airplane Company of Seattle had a branch in Vancouver. "I think he only had a Grade Eight education," says his son. "It was strictly a

129

financial thing and a sad thing to see. I'm sure he wondered, like the rest of us, what he might have done with a little more formal education."

With the example of his father's limited career to spur him on, John Madden made an intense dedication to higher education, earning a Master of Science degree in nuclear physics from the University of British Columbia and then going to Oxford for his doctorate. He spent three years in England, from 1961 to 1964, but even twenty years later his voice retains a studied Oxford intonation. There can be no mistaking that John Madden is an educated man.

At Oxford, he worked with computers as a part of his studies in nuclear physics, and upon his return to Canada, Madden went to work for Computing Devices of Canada in Ottawa, deciding that his peripheral academic interest in computing, and not nuclear physics, would be the focus of his career. "There was a lot of debate in those days about the brain drain south and a similar debate about how little research and development was done in industry. It would have been very easy for me to get a job teaching physics in a university, and it was very strange for someone with a doctorate to go and work in industry," he explains. Madden stayed with Computing Devices for five years and rose to become the company's chief research engineer.

He moved on to the federal Communications Research Centre west of Ottawa. At that time, British and French engineers were developing videotex systems and by 1975 Britain had a functioning public system called Prestel. At Communications Research Centre, meanwhile, Canadian engineers were experimenting with the transmission of computer graphics by telephone line, a difficult and comparatively slow method because of the line's restricted capacity. A telephone line cannot, for example, contain the flow of information necessary to transmit a moving television image. "It wasn't terribly directed research," Madden recalls. The Hospital for Sick Children in Toronto did want some way of displaying graphic symbols for the deaf and other handicapped people and the Canadian military wanted a means of communicating maps and diagrams, and the researchers were trying to satisfy those needs rather than come up with a videotex system for mass distribution. The actual invention of Telidon is credited to Herb Bown, a government engineer from Newfoundland. Bown now works for Norpak in Kanata, which has

130

bet its whole existence on an eventual mass market for Telidon hardware and manufactures adapters that turn Apple II home computers into Telidon terminals.

Essentially, the Canadian technology called Telidon consists less of machines than of software. Telidon is a set of computer codes that can be transmitted by either a telephone line or a television broadcast signal. The television receiver interprets the codes and generates images on the screen. The resulting words and graphics can be useful aids to adult students learning at home – or they can be merely another vehicle for commercial advertising.

Telidon's development has been dominated by a partnership of engineers and marketeers. Engineers are prone to infatuation with the how of a new technology, without pondering whether it has a why. Marketeers seize upon new communications technologies as vehicles for advertising. Telidon had no one on its side who had a practical plan to endow it with a usefulness obvious to a mass of citizens. As as result, most Telidon systems are about as attractive as the Yellow Pages.

Telidon is, in fact, a perfect example of need creation in which promoters lose money and hype upon the population in a bombardment intended to shake out a presumed but hitherto unfelt demand. "A solution in search of a problem" has become a commonplace epithet among computer industry leaders sceptical of Telidon's value. Of all the technologies with their roots in Canadian innovation, Telidon is the most difficult to assess. The discourse of Telidon proponents is such a mix of fact and futuristic fantasy that it is obvious that the entire Telidon community has lost contact with time and reality. It functions in a bizarre atmosphere of government grants, cigar-sucking executives in three-piece pinstripe suits posing as fomenters of social revolution, and wild promises of millions to be made from this silent, still-picture version of television. Telidon systems will probably find niches among the electronic media, but it is increasingly obvious that these roles will be much more modest and mundane than the prophets of a wired world have promised.

The Telidon images emerge on the home screen for all the world like paint-by-numbers work in progress. What saves Telidon from being merely sluggish, fuzzy television is that viewers can select the individual screens, or "pages," of information and graphics they want and hold each one like a projected slide until they are ready for more. These pages, identified by numbers, are indexed in a printed directory or on master Telidon images called menus.

There are two distinct ways of transmitting Telidon pages. One, called videotex, involves linking the television set by a telephone line or other wire to a central computer where the codes to give each page shape and colour are stored on magnetic disks. The information seeker uses a small keypad wired to his television to call for the desired page. The request travels, from the viewer's fingertips, down the telephone line to the storage computer, which finds the page and then sends its stream of coded electrical pulses back over the line to a decoder in the television set, which then displays the requested page. In such a videotex system, thousands of pages can be at the viewer's beck and call.

The second means of distributing Telidon images is to broadcast their codes together with a normal television signal. If the viewer were to have total individual control over his choice of pages he would require a broadcast transmitter of his own to signal to the Telidon computer which page he wanted to see. The computer would then have to transmit a specific set of codes to that specific television set, creating an impossible jumble of broadcast signals. Instead, the Telidon broadcast signal carries a repeating cycle of encoded pages, about 125 in all. The page cycle continues like a carousel, with each page returning every dozen seconds. By choosing a page number from a keypad that looks like a remote control channel selector, the viewer can tell his own Telidon decoder to snag a specific page as it passes through the airwaves on its cycle and then produce that page on the screen. This use of broadcasting to deliver Telidon pages is called teletext.*

---

*Videotex means Telidon or similar systems which deliver their information by telephone line and permit the user to control the central computer through his own keyboard or keypad. A confusing lexicon has evolved to denote the various marriages of computer and communications technologies. Teletext means the broadcasting of Telidon or similar graphic images. Drop the final t, and it becomes Teletex, which is the transmission of letters or messages from one computer or word processor to another over special networks. Similarly, videotex means Telidon or its competing systems delivered by telephone line while, with the t, videotext means the transmission of textual information from a central computer through telephone lines to home or office computers.

The evolution to a computerized society has been called "technology driven" because, often, the new machines are introduced before the need for them is felt. Telidon, however, was politically driven. It emerged from the government laboratory just as Bell Canada was undertaking a videotex system using British Prestel technology. Ontario's educational television network had its own plans to test France's Antiope teletext system. The spectre of proliferating videotex systems that could not communicate with each other was abhorrent to the neat, bureaucratic minds within the federal department of communications. The guardians of the public good also perceived their chance to sound an alarm of cultural invasion, always a sure means of exciting politicians trained in the national tradition of protectionism and timidity.

Madden and Canada's mandarin par excellence, Bernard Ostry, who was deputy minister of communications, twisted arms and bent ears up and down the chain of command until they got their first chunk of money, $9 million, to sow the seeds of Telidon. "Bernie Ostry knew a lot of people and worked very hard at that," says Madden. "And I guess I knew a number of people too. It was certainly possible, if not easy, to get access to some fairly influential people and get them briefed. The reason why there was some urgency to it was that other countries were substantially subsidizing and promoting their own videotex systems. The option that we seemed to be faced with was either going ahead with a Canadian system, which looked to be much better and which had a chance of becoming a standard, or lying back and letting everybody buy French, British, American, Japanese, or goodness knows what equipment."

The ideological justification went beyond the balance of payments and the desirability of standardization. Madden became a Telidon proselytizer, arguing that the new communications technology could enhance democracy itself. "I think the major social benefit is access to information. Concomitant with that, one would assume, is an opening up of society. People would have a better idea of what was going on and therefore be able to change things in a more informed and enlightened way."

All would depend, according to Madden's vision of the near future in "Julia's Dilemma," on how information technology would be controlled, and by whom. In Julia's Canada of the first decade of the next

133

century, programming of AYEEs had become the dominant industry. "AYEE development had proceeded without regulation, not because the dangers were not foreseen but because no one could reach agreement on what the specific dangers and remedies were. In the meantime, enormous fortunes were made in AYEE manufacture by a few large corporations, and the profits had been used to acquire control of much of the rest of the world's economy."

Given Madden's pessimistic fictional assessment of how the profit motive could subvert the beneficial potential of new information technologies, his department's actual choice of allies – first AT&T and then a combine of presumably competing newspaper publishers – to establish Telidon as a world standard is strangely ironic. "It was a very key part of the strategy," Madden confides, "to convince AT&T that if we didn't have a North American standard we were all in trouble."

The strategy worked – almost too well. AT&T allowed that Telidon was the best but felt that it could be even better. The system AT&T envisaged would be able to convert graphics transmitted by the European systems and would increase the capabilities of Telidon itself. And the American company didn't particularly like the name Telidon, which had been concocted by a Canadian government researcher from ancient Greek words meaning "distant" and "to see." AT&T gave its videotex specifications the stark label "North American Presentation Level Protocol Syntax" whose acronym is NAPLPS, sometimes deliciously pronounced "naplips."

The Canadians had previously considered making the improvements that AT&T now demanded, but their system was already the most complex in the international standards competition. "AT&T forced us willingly, I guess, is the best way to put it," says Madden. But the resulting North American standard, while based on Telidon, required substantial modification to the Canadian system, giving competitors in other countries time to catch up, and Madden admits "it really just kind of tied the whole thing up in knots for about twelve to eighteen months while we all adjusted. The change in standard essentially brought things to a halt. That, and the fact that the economic downturn caused the market to develop rather more slowly than a lot of people had estimated, is giving our competitors – I mean not so much the British and the French as the Americans and the Japanese – a chance to get their minds around our standard. And so, as we've always been predicting, we're into a nose-to-nose struggle with the big guys. The question then is how much of the equipment is going to be Canadian."

About twenty companies in the United States, Japan, France, and Canada are making Telidon receivers. The Canadian firms are Microtel, Norpak, Northern Telecom, and Electrohome, but few of their machines are yet visible, even in Canada. The closest thing to mass contact between Canadians and Telidon comes through terminals made by Microtel and Norpak spotted around Toronto as part of an advertising and information system called Teleguide, which provides tourist information and advertising to pedestrians. The first big Telidon videotex system to use the new North American standard, Teleguide is run by Infomart, the *Toronto Star*-Southam venture which, with the help of a $600,000 grant from Ottawa, has become the leading international purveyor of videotex software and systems.

Infomart operates from a squat, futuristic building in Toronto that looks as if it should be either an outpost on Mars or an undersea research station. After the *Globe and Mail* pulled out of the venture in 1979 and the two remaining publishers pushed ahead with plans to try out Telidon, they hired an Albertan named David Carlisle to become Infomart's president. Carlisle ran Infomart until his firing in August 1983 as a result of disagreement with the publishers over Telidon's value as a mass medium. He had not become Canada's pivotal Telidon player because of personal charm. He didn't bother to hide, even from a first-time visitor, his bristling impatience with the work of his own staff. Carlisle's pleasure in high position was manifest in his precise manipulation of cigars of a length and thickness that went out of fashion with the railway barons. He combs his hair, René Lévesque style, laterally across a bare crown. The skin of his head is drawn tightly over a severely sculptured skull whose spacious cranium and perfect jaw line might well satisfy an extraterrestrial conception of what a human head should look like.

David Carlisle's laugh erupts in loud short bursts without apparent cause for humour. These laughs invariably punctuated Carlisle's explanations of how Infomart would crush any competition and made vast fortunes for its patrons. Carlisle's intense laughs don't trail away; they end abruptly as though some inner digital clock had commanded the face to return instantly to its normal, brooding expression.

135

Carlisle, born in 1936, was raised at Grande Prairie in northern Alberta's Peace River country. He studied electrical engineering at the University of Alberta and after graduating in 1958 went to England for three years of study and part-time work in electronics. Returning to Canada in 1961, he joined IBM first as a systems engineer in Edmonton, finishing his career with the company as marketing manager in Ottawa in 1969. He was one of the three founding executives in 1971 of Datacrown, which within five years became the largest computer service bureau in Canada. Carlisle had both the experience and the drive to make him attractive to worried newspaper executives who, in the late 1970s, were at the same time fascinated and frightened by the notion of electronic publishing.

Carlisle hired a crew of forty programmers to improve the Communications Research Centre's original Telidon software. "Very expensive guys" is how Carlisle described the Infomart software engineers who earn up to $60,000 annually. By January 1980, Infomart had both a computer and page creation terminals in operation. That spring, Infomart participated in the first field test of Telidon, which took place in the Manitoba farming community of South Headingly. Twenty rural families were given Telidon terminals for the trial, followed in 1981 by 150 more in Elie, Manitoba, where, for the first time, telephone and Telidon signals travelled to subscribers' homes as blips of laser light through optical fibre.

Manitoba was confirmed as the test area for Telidon when Infomart opened an office with its own computer installation in Winnipeg. Infomart's Winnipeg operation provided Canada's first commercial videotex service, called Grassroots, in 1982. Farmers, from the start of efforts to make a paying proposition of videotex, had been identified as the most obvious potential clients for an instant information service. Daily and even hourly farm activities depend on weather and market conditions, so that information has an immediate and obvious economic worth to farmers. Farmers also make up a neatly defined target audience for the potential advertisers who, according to Infomart's grand scheme, would be the arms suppliers of the information revolution. By pushing the right buttons on their remote control keypads, Prairie farmers can even summon to their television screen a colourful weather map of the Russian steppes and check on the fortunes of the competition in the race to supply bread for the Soviet belly. Branded, in yellow, upon the Ural Mountains is the globe-pawing lion of the Royal Bank of Canada, sponsor of the weather in Russia.

In its second year of operation, Grassroots was delivering Telidon pages to 1,100 subscribers who pay the Manitoba Telephone System fifty dollars a month for the rental of their terminals and five cents for each minute they are connected by the phone lines to Infomart's Winnipeg computers. David Carlisle qualified Grassroots as "quite a successful business," but that did not imply that it is profitable. Profitability remains one innovation elusive to the entire videotex industry.

In contrast to Carlisle, who insisted a few months before his dismissal that Infomart would eventually make a lot of money, his interim successor, William Hutchison, dismisses the importance of profit as a motive behind the venture. "Infomart is really an R&D vehicle of the two publishers," says Hutchison. "When people ask when Infomart will become profitable, I answer, 'Well, when is Bell-Northern Research going to be profitable?' Who cares? That's not the objective. Infomart is a research exercise by these two major publishers who want to understand the way the world is going."

In January 1982, Infomart joined the Times Mirror Company, publisher of the *Los Angeles Times*, in a joint venture called Videotex America. Its objective is to dominate videotex operations in cities throughout the United States, and Videotex America's first commercial videotex service was to be launched in mid-1984 in Los Angeles after a market test in 350 Southern California homes. That 1982 field trial has assured Videotex America that people are ready for home shopping, banking, news delivery, games, and electronic mail provided by Telidon videotex. The Los Angeles service will provide, initially, fifty thousand pages of videotex information and advertising. Not surprisingly, given Infomart's own parentage, Videotex America seeks partnerships with newspaper publishers in its target markets. Agreements to pursue videotex projects have been signed with the publishers of the *San Francisco Chronicle*, the *Arizona Republic*, and the *Jacksonville Journal*.

In Canada, Infomart has not yet attempted to establish a home videotex system, but in September 1982 the company started the Teleguide system. Its terminals are peppered about shopping malls and other public areas in the city and look, according to a writer in *Saturday Night*, "like television sets perched on garbage cans." Infomart has spent $14 million on Teleguide. In what is simply a direct subsidy to the advertising industry, the federal government chipped in another $2 million to pay for the Electrohome and Microtel terminals. Tourist information plus restaurant and consumer advertising make up Teleguide's bank of Telidon pages.

Disappointment with Teleguide both as a commercial venture and as an attractive service contributed to the general disillusionment with Telidon technology on the part of the newspaper companies. One of Southam's Infomart directors admits that even he abandoned trying to retrieve the information he was seeking from a Teleguide terminal in a Toronto shopping mall. Robert McConnell, a Southam vice-president, was looking for the location of paint and wallpaper stores after moving from Montreal, where he had been publisher of the *Gazette*. He gave up and turned in frustration to the shopping centre's old-fashioned store directory mounted on the wall. The Teleguide system, he complains, "was too damned slow and I found myself going round in circles." Infomart's owners are unsure of Teleguide's future. "There's one line of thought that says Teleguide can be developed into a viable business," says McConnell. "There's another opinion that Teleguide is really a starter set that we can learn from but that will eventually have to be discarded."

McConnell describes himself as "a media man" used to dealing with people "who want something and are willing to pay for it." The proponents of Telidon, on the other hand, argue that after the consuming public has been properly educated about the wondrous advantages of videotex, they will begin to purchase terminals and subscribe to home services. "It doesn't sound like a natural sell to me," says a sceptical McConnell. The publishers have come to realize, he says, that Telidon will not penetrate homes like radio, television, or the old daily paper itself. "Everybody has now concluded that videotex is not in any foreseeable future a replacement for newspapers or any other mass medium."

Part of the reason for Telidon's redundancy as a useful public medium may be Infomart's purposeful smudging of the distinction between information and advertising. Advertising, on Telidon, becomes "purchasing information" in company Newspeak, while

138

advertisers themselves are called information providers. The suggestion that Teleguide is just a collection of ads riled Carlisle. "This is a new medium and we do things a different way," he insisted, drawing on the barbarous lexicon of the Information Age. "There's lots of massification in advertising, lots of noise." Teleguide's contents may look like newspaper or magazine ads, but to Carlisle they have a higher purpose. "It's not advertising anymore, dammit. It's information."

Carlisle's fusion of information and advertising would have entertained Marshall McLuhan. In *Understanding Media*'s famous chapter "The Medium is the Message," he wrote, "It is only today that industries have become aware of the various kinds of business in which they are engaged. When IBM discovered that it was not in the business of making office equipment or business machines, but that it was in the business of processing information, then it began to navigate with clear vision."

Telidon's disappointing development as a successful business or a socially useful medium may find its explanation in McLuhan's analysis. The thrust of their joint venture in Infomart indicates that the big newspaper publishers decided that they are not in the news or information business after all, but are instead in the advertising business.

With Infomart as its chosen instrument in the videotex version of Telidon that uses telephone lines to connect terminals to the central computer, Ottawa made the Canadian Broadcasting Corporation its privileged vehicle for the broadcast, or teletext, version of the technology. Here, at least, the rhetoric was modest and more appropriate to Telidon's true contribution to communications. The government in 1981 gave the CBC $6 million to set up experimental teletext projects on both its English channels and its French network, Radio-Canada. The CBC was to transmit the Telidon codes as part of its usual television broadcast signal. They could be carried with the part of the signal that normally produces the solid black line (the vertical blanking interval) just above the picture, visible to a viewer who fiddles with the horizontal hold control of the television set. Much of the money allocated for the experiment had to be spent on Telidon receiving equipment to be placed in the homes of the five hundred families selected at random to be its instant audience.

Project Iris was the name the CBC chose for its Telidon trial. Iris, a sea nymph of Greek mythology, was the gods' messenger between heaven and earth, and her passage was marked by the rainbow. In one of its more enlightened moves, and in contrast to the choice of Infomart's newspaper publishers, the CBC called in not a computer expert but a veteran newsman to set up its Montreal teletext centre. Jean-Claude Asselin knew nothing about computers, but he knew news.

At first sight, Jean-Claude Asselin makes you think of a tourist caught in a revolution. Around him, dressed in the revolution's uniform of jeans and jogging shoes, young men and women are tapping away at keyboards, confecting new electronic pages of text and pictures for the wall of shimmering television monitors of this dimly lit, basement corner of the Radio-Canada headquarters in downtown Montreal. Asselin among these young artists of the electronic palette is an anachronism with his roly-poly middle-aged torso shrink-wrapped by a shirt of shiny blue polyester. He looks exactly what he is, an old-fashioned newspaperman who remembers vividly the days when pages weren't "created" at terminals but were hammered, cursed, and clamped into place by sweaty men working with trays of lead castings laid on long steel tables called stones.

Asselin began his newspapering a quarter-century ago the way many journalism careers still start – rewriting other reporters' stories for the wires of Canadian Press. Later, he was an editor with the now defunct Montreal tabloid called *La Patrie* and then with the daily *La Presse*. Asselin made his first technological leap by joining Radio-Canada in 1970 and, for a dozen years, organized television coverage of special events like space shots and elections. When the CBC asked him to implement its experimental Telidon service, it was, in some ways, a step backward in skills and specialties for Asselin. The old tricks of the newspaper desk were more relevant to this new technology than were the techniques of television, despite the fact that superficially Telidon resembles television.

"We were told that Telidon was the best system in the world, better than the British, better than the French," recalls Asselin. Then, with his forefinger he tugs down his lower eyelid in the French-Canadian gesture meaning "my eye." "The only trouble with it was that it didn't work."

140

In its first tests in August 1982, the CBC discovered that all the cable companies whose signals it tested were cheating on the quality of the signal they were feeding to subscribers' homes. They were boosting it by means inexpensive and inconsequential as far as the normal television image was concerned, but in the process they were destroying the capacity of the vertical blanking interval to carry Telidon code. Just as bad, the manufacturers of Telidon equipment and software were in the midst of converting to the North American standard decreed by AT&T, and the systems available to the CBC were a mishmash of old and new. So Asselin rolled up his newspaperman's sleeves and went to work, recruiting CBC programmers from their regular duties and taking advantage of the mess to infuse his journalistic experience into the building of a usable broadcast version of Telidon.

When Telidon code started flowing in a stream of white dots across the vertical blanking interval in April 1983, Asselin's work was visible in the design of the resulting pages. He wanted Telidon pages to be created in the same way newspaper pages are laid out – with the ads and logos already blocked out before the remaining space, the news hole, is turned over to the editors to be filled. On this principle, Asselin used Telidon's ability to leave titles and layout design intact while other parts of the page displayed on the television screen were changed as the viewer turns from one page to another.

Project Iris was to run for several months while the CBC decided whether it would continue to broadcast pages of Telidon information at a predicted cost of $2 million a year. Technically, at least, it was largely a success though hardly a revolution. The noble vision of Telidon as a personal encyclopedia and democracy machine has so far materialized, in the case of Teleguide, as an electronic carrier boy stuffing digital advertising flyers into electronic garbage cans or, with Project Iris, as visible radio. "We are," concludes Asselin, "the fast food of the information business."

CHAPTER SEVEN

The Soft Part Begins

On rare clear winter mornings before the sun has scaled the Coast Range, the lights of Grouse Mountain's ski slopes float freely in the black sky like the cast-off necklace of some divine temptress. Below, the city of Vancouver twinkles with the headlights of cars crossing bridges and ships slowly moving through inlets and harbours. It's this scene of sensuous promise that starts the days, or at least the rainless days, of Canada's biggest promotor of software ventures. Tarrnie Williams has made his name in the business not by the wildfire success of his programs but by his ingenious methods of financing them.

Tall, good-looking, and wearing the enigmatic smirk of a riverboat gambler, Williams is a smooth talker who managed to convert a muffin company into a software factory and set up shop in an expansive indoor jungle of tropical plants and attractive young workers who divide their gaze between the mountains presiding over the city and the screens of their IBM terminals. They sometimes work out their problems by writing on the walls, which Williams thoughtfully had constructed of erasable white panels from ceiling to floor. There's little of the hum and jangle of the usual open-plan office – just the rhythmic clicking of keyboards.

In five fast years, Williams built Sydney Development Corporation into a staff of two hundred programmers and salesmen in Canada, England, and the United States with revenues of $11.6 million. To help do this, he invited investors to give their tax money to him instead of to the government.

Williams got his business start selling mutual fund subscriptions in Montreal for Bernie Cornfeld's Investors Overseas Services. That was in the mid-1960s, when Cornfeld was still the Pavarotti of the investment world, before he conned bankers, pension fund managers, and other suckers of high finance in the world's greatest multimillion-dollar fraud. In Canada, IOS was permitted by the government to sell only the conservative, well-managed Dreyfus Fund, and Williams is sure his clients did well from the investments he sold them. And so did Williams, with a clientele including not only the standard doctors and lawyers but also a group of professionals that most investment sellers would neither think of nor dare approach in daylight.

Williams specialized in selling financial security to the strippers who worked in the bars along St. Catherine Street and St. Lawrence Street. Montreal's strip clubs open early while the city's proper demoiselles are just taking their first coffee breaks from their office desks. Tarrnie spent the daylight hours in the darkness of those clubs, talking to the women. "They make good money, and mutual funds are a very good method of saving when you have a good income, haven't the foggiest idea of money matters, and may not be overly bright."

When he wasn't selling mutual funds, Williams spent his time editing a book written by a university friend who was one of the earliest experts in a new technique of project management called critical path, whose purpose Williams defines simply as "completing a project on time, on budget." Editing the text gave Williams some competence himself in critical path management, and there was, in 1966, a project at hand in dire need of methodical control. Preparations for Montreal's Expo 67 world's fair were in a mess, and Williams was hired as one of the dozens of Expo project managers trying to wrest order from chaos. That experience was also Williams's first with computers. IBM was installing machines throughout the Expo site, both as exhibits and as control systems, and Williams was the project manager responsible for several of them.

Expo was also the setting for his romance with Penny Hemsworth, a daughter of Vancouver's free wheeling financial community. She had no difficulty, after the big fair was over, convincing her new husband that the West Coast was where he should be.

Williams applied on a Friday for a job at IBM's Vancouver office, and on Monday, he was back east again in Toronto for a six-week company course. He spent nine years with IBM as a systems engineer, salesman, and trainer and cemented his expertise in computers and project management. Then, after two years with the Insurance Corporation of British Columbia applying principles of project management to the government insurance agency's computer operations, Williams was ready to strike out on his own.

He decided, in 1978, to build a business based on his experience in the computerization of project management. To do that he needed money. That obstacle was not as daunting for Williams as it is for aspirant entrepreneurs without his connections. His wife's father had founded a Vancouver brokerage firm, and Penny's brother, who calls himself "H. Barry Hemsworth the Magnificent," is a Vancouver lawyer. Like many of his colleagues of the B.C. bar, he's also a stock promoter.

His family relationships had previously led Williams to dabble in the adventurous Vancouver capital markets. He invested in and became a director of a company called Cheyenne Petroleum, which was listed on the Vancouver Stock Exchange along with dozens of other speculative exploration companies. It was this gamble in oil that led Williams into muffins, and then into software. As he explains it, "Cheyenne got into the embarrassing position of actually finding a major gas field. So we had the job of taking the development dollars we had been able to raise and turning it into a producing company."

First, the company had to consolidate its claim by buying up adjoining claims in British Columbia's Grizzly Valley, near Chetwynd, northeast of Vancouver. One of these was held by another Hemsworth holding, New Chief Mines, which, in the complex life of such companies, had been reorganized into something called Sydney Development Corporation. This company had been listed on the stock exchange as an oil company but was then withdrawn from trading while Williams's brother-in-law prepared to turn it into a franchiser of muffin stores. Sydney was the name of the daughter of one of the company's previous owners.

"They progressed fairly far along until they went to the fellow who in fact had the recipes, and he decided that he didn't want to become the Colonel Sanders of the muffin business," recounts Williams. Williams saw potential in the muffinless muffin company. Its chief attraction was that it had already gone through the lengthy and expensive

145

process of getting listed on the stock exchange. Instead of becoming a muffin company, it would become a computer company, Williams decided.

He traded some of his interest in the Grizzly Valley gas field for control of Sydney and spent $5,000 of his own money for a management consultant's feasibility study which confirmed that his plan was a sound one. Williams proposed to shareholders of the virtually worthless firm that it be reorganized under his management. Sydney shareholders concurred, and, on May 10, 1978, Sydney Development was relisted on the Vancouver Stock Exchange at thirty-six cents a share, under Williams's control, with declared assets of $60,000 worth of Cheyenne Petroleum shares.

Now Williams had to find a means of taking his knowledge of project management and turning it into a computer program package that could work for a variety of business and government customers. Williams himself was not a programmer. He hired two green computer science graduates from the University of British Columbia and two more from the British Columbia Institute of Technology and set them to work constructing the program he had already named Connect II. There never was a Connect I, but in the frenetic computer business where products are rushed into the market before they are fit, buyers may distrust initial versions of anything. The most popular of the personal computer data base programs is called dBase II, though no dBase I had ever existed. Labelling something as version II gives it an apparent ancestry and heritage of technical refinement.

To pay for the software development in 1978, Williams leap-frogged the Rockies to Calgary, a city then heady with oil wealth and celebrated for multimillion-dollar deals closed before breakfast on a handshake. Williams knew the language of the oil men. "In selling Sydney, I used the analogy of oil: that developing software is no different from drilling a well." With the help of Tony Suche, a Calgary oil promoter, he raised $180,000 from twenty-five petroleum players, reassured by Sydney's shares in Cheyenne. "They understood that if Sydney didn't work as a computer company, it could always become an oil company again."

Connect II was developed far more quickly than Williams had anticipated thanks to Lee Moller, the first young programmer he had hired. Williams paid him from a federal grant awarded to encourage innovative product design. The design grant was really meant for things like furniture and clever kitchen utensils, but Williams convinced Ottawa that the design of a new computer program could be as elegant and rewarding for Canadian trade as another fancy table.

When Williams first hired Moller, the eager young programmer arrived at work neatly turned out in suit and tie. Today, wealthy for his twenty-seven years, Moller is more relaxed and wears his jeans casually tucked into high leather boots. He looks out to the mountains through aviator glasses and a gold chain shows between the front panels of his shirt, which is unbuttoned to the midriff. His thick blond hair is parted in the centre. Perched atop the monitor of his computer terminal is a pair of binoculars – standard gear in Vancouver for anyone whose office has a view – and the white helmet he wears when tearing about town on his Suzuki 850. Moller makes $35,000 a year programming for Sydney Development. Through the company's employee stock option plan he has also managed to collect about twenty-five thousand Sydney shares, which were worth well over $100,000 in early 1983 when Moller was scouting for a house to purchase at Whistler Mountain. He eventually shared in the purchase of a luxurious $200,000 ski retreat with three others, including Tarrnie Williams.

Programming pays well and can have its whimsical moments. Between Sydney's programmers and the mountains, the Granville Street Bridge provides a pattern of constant motion over the ripple of False Creek. The steady flow of traffic was broken one day when a bus caught fire as it was crossing, causing commotion on the bridge and inspiration among the programmers. One of them, Jay Mac-Donald, duplicated the scene on his terminal, with orange tips of flame dancing from his electronic bus. Then the whole group got carried away with MacDonald's video game, adding runners who raced across the bridge and could be hit or missed by the burning bus. A dive bomber suddenly appeared to decrease the poor runners' chances. Things worsened further for the joggers with the addition of shell-firing tanks, flying bats, trees, and fire hydrants that would materialize at unpredictable times and places. "People don't like us to run this too much," says Moller. "It really drags the machine into the ground."

Williams himself, however, has decided that games may be a lucrative use for the computer and in 1983 issued a special stock offering to

147

Sydney shareholders to finance a separate Sydney games division. Sydney's first game success was Evolution, a graphics game invented by Vancouver teenagers Don Mattrick and Jeff Sember whom Williams paid with shares in Sydney and continuing royalties. Williams stipulated in the royalty contract that before receiving any cash they had to set aside in trust from their earnings enough money to finance their university educations. That accomplished within months, each now drives his own expensive Japanese sports car, paid for in cash. (Williams himself drives a Volkswagen Rabbit.)

Moller's Connect II, which was designed for IBM mainframes, was first installed in 1979 on a trial basis on the computers of B.C. Hydro, the Insurance Corporation of British Columbia, and the Manitoba government. It worked, and the test clients decided to pay for the program. The reserves were now proven, and Williams had to pump oil and build a pipeline to bring it to market. Sydney issued more stock and hired a flying squad of salesmen to sell Connect II. But with only one product and few sales, Sydney barely survived 1980.

Pressed by the need to generate revenue, Williams began buying up small Vancouver and American firms with promising programs of their own. These acquisitions, rather than original program creation, would become Sydney's immediate source of commercially successful software. By early 1983, Sydney had acquired five other software firms and their programs. Williams has managed to do it all without actually paying cash for the companies he acquires. He takes them over in exchange for a few tradeable shares in Sydney itself and a promise of more if the former owners stay with the company as division managers and attain profit targets set down in the sale contract. If they fail, Sydney keeps the extra stock.

Williams's best financing coup was creation of Canada's first public software tax shelter in 1981. He made clever use of income tax incentives for scientific research and development, which can actually net the wealthy investor more in tax write-offs than he invests. Investors, in effect, pay part of their taxes to private promoters instead of to the public treasury. Ottawa introduced the tax shelter scheme to encourage spending on scientific research by permitting taxpayers to deduct their R&D investments from their taxable income and claim an additional tax credit of up to 10 per cent of that investment. The net effect is that a taxpayer who invests $10,000 in an R&D tax shelter

148

pays only $4,550 for his share in the research project. The other $5,450 would have gone to the government if it hadn't been sheltered.

Williams was the first businessman to define software development as scientific research and secure from the federal revenue department what is called an advance tax ruling, assuring prospective investors that their claims for deductions will be accepted. He had personal experience with tax shelters in the 1970s, including an oil well, an apartment building, and a movie. To encourage the Canadian cinema, Ottawa had passed a law declaring private investment in Canadian-made movies to be deductible from taxable revenue. That generated a flurry of investment activity and a blizzard of bad movies. Williams had invested in one called *Death Ship* but missed its three-day run in Vancouver.

He laughs about the experience. "I felt rather badly about that, being a 0.6-per-cent investor in the horrendous cost of *Death Ship*. Fortunately, when I was in San Francisco about six months later, I noticed it was playing in a triple bill. I saw the tail end of something or other, and then an MC got up on the stage and pulled ten tickets out of a hat for a give-away of dishes. Then up came *Death Ship* with George Kennedy. It was bad, but not *that* bad. So I saw my movie, the most expensive movie I've ever paid to see: twenty-five grand."

To Williams's mind, "a movie is basically the same as software – it's ideas on celluloid." So, inspired by the financing of *Death Ship*, he put together Sydney's first tax shelter offering in 1981 and netted nearly eight million dollars by promising to spend the money on program development so that investors could claim their share as a tax deduction.

As Parliament had intended, the tax shelter scheme was putting high-tech minds to work, though in Sydney's case it was in the development of software rather than of hardware as the legislators had probably anticipated. If Sydney had stuck to its plan to make muffins, there would have been little fuss with the tax men. Muffins they would see and understand. What Williams was trying to sell seemed about as tangible as mist in the moonlight. But it was increasingly obvious, outside of the revenue department, that software holds as much hope as a profitable export for Canada as does computer equipment itself. There was no displeasure with Williams's use of the tax shelter – except among the tax collectors. Sydney's successful tax shelter had coincided with another even bigger scheme by Northern Telecom which made it possible for other private business firms to deduct the equivalent of 150 per cent of their investments in Northern's research from their corporate taxes. Unlike Sydney Development's purely software projects, Northern Telecom's research did involve hardware development. Northern was clearly within the law, but in the minds of some revenue officials it had abused the spirit of the tax shelter by giving corporations instead of individuals an opportunity to invest in another company's research projects. The investing corporations were able to benefit not only from the tax shelter but also from another federal tax provision that let them claim deductions for having increased their R&D spending over the previous year's.

Stirred up by the successes of Northern and Sydney in diverting millions from the federal treasury, the revenue department divided into warring camps. The faction accepting the government's clear intention of encouraging high-tech by means of the tax shelters was blocked by an old guard of dour, sanctimonious tax deacons whose fundamentalist principles just couldn't tolerate having the government's due revenues splurged on intangible schemes to benefit the sort of investor who drives a BMW or Mercedes.

The dispute literally caused the gears of the revenue department to seize, with the result that during most of 1982, officials simply refused to issue rulings on what would qualify as a research and development tax shelter in the computer industry. The stern mouth puckerers of the revenue department dug in and resisted the impotent wrath of cabinet ministers who learned of the bureaucrats' moratorium from angry businessmen. The politicians were more concerned with the urgency of supporting high-tech development than they were about possible inequities of tax breaks.

Sentiment regarding Sydney's successes with tax shelters is mixed even within the software industry, which stands to benefit from them. "They're just spending the government's money. Their investors are the kind of people who would rather throw their money in the river than pay taxes," snorted Rod Bryden, once a senior civil servant himself and now chairman and president of Canada's biggest computer software firm, Systemhouse of Ottawa.

Bryden's quick pronouncement on the propriety of tax shelters seemed a little less convincing when he later confided that he too had tried – but failed – to secure a precious advance tax ruling like the one so beneficial to Sydney. But Bryden appears to have trouble resisting opportunities for interesting controversy. His calm voice and gentlemanly demeanour mask an apparent joy in saying the outrageous.

Roderick Bryden has managed to run Systemhouse without ever using a computer. He is an engaging, thoroughly likeable man with a wry smile constantly prying at the corners of his lips. He speaks softly but confidently like a man accustomed to controversy and sure that, occasionally, he may be right when everyone else is wrong.

Bryden was born in 1941 on a farm near Shemogue, New Brunswick, the son of Scottish immigrants. He married his high school sweetheart, Georgia Marie Estabrooks, and started a family precociously enough to be a grandfather by the time he was thirty-seven. After studying economics and law in New Brunswick and Michigan, he taught law at the University of Saskatchewan in Saskatoon where the dean was a rare prairie Liberal named Otto Lang. Bryden managed Lang's successful campaign for election to Parliament in 1968 and then followed him to Ottawa as his special assistant. Lang's first cabinet responsibility was grain.

There was a dramatic surplus of wheat on the prairies that year and it meant financial crisis for farmers. Bryden was put in charge of an ad hoc Grains Group staffed from several departments. He came up with a policy called LIFT, a typical government double-think acronym meaning Lower Inventories for Tomorrow. Farmers were paid cash for *not* growing wheat, and supply fell back in line with demand. "It's the kind of thing any business but farming would do automatically," Bryden says. "But in a world where people are hungry, it's a very difficult moral problem to decide not to grow grain, to intentionally leave land out of production."

Next, he moved with his minister to the Department of Manpower and Immigration where he became national director of a winter employment scheme called the Local Initiatives Program. At the time, in 1972, taking potshots at government giveaways to hippies, homosexuals, and leftists was the preferred sport of press gallery reporters who sniffed every handout like drug-tracking dogs in search of public subsidization of sexual or political perversion. But Quebec's October

Crisis was only two years behind, and the jeers of the media were minor irritants compared with the Trudeau government's fear of sparks of violence in tinder-dry pockets of severe unemployment. Bryden was told to spend money in a hurry. "The real value of the job was not whether the church got painted but whether the individual maintained his positive attitude through a very bad winter, so that by the next spring he was still working and paying his way in society and hadn't given up and said, 'To hell with it.' " Each morning, Bryden and two other program officials went over the proposals transmitted overnight by Telex from regional offices. In just a few weeks they spent $90 million. "That was great fun," Bryden says. "I enjoyed that. Quite a productive experience."

Bryden concluded his public service career at the bull's eye of another target of media arrows, the Department of Regional Economic Expansion. It looked like the biggest pork barrel of all time, dipped into for millions by corporations whose promises to create jobs in one part of the country often turned out to mean the elimination of dozens more in another province. He became an assistant deputy minister and was charged with restructuring the department's operations.

Bryden quit government at the end of 1973 to satisfy a nagging urge to set up a business of his own. "I left government with a great deal of experience, some sense of knowledge about how the government process works, and no money at all," he remembers. "On a net worth basis I was probably negative $15,000." Business appealed to him because of the freedom it seemed to offer. "It's unstructured. You're constrained only by the resources you can muster and by the talent of the people you can convince to work with you." Unlike working in government service, he thought, he could function in anonymity. "You don't have to bother reading the *Globe and Mail* every morning to see if they like what you do." This, Bryden would later learn when Systemhouse got into trouble, is not quite the case once a businessman invites public investment and comes under the scrutiny of not only the press but also powerful analysts who work for brokerage firms and advise investors on the worth of a particular enterprise. But at the time, compared to the fluorescent glare of public life, business promised refuge. Besides, Bryden considered that business just might provide better expression for his commitment to the public good. "There were a great many people quite prepared to be in the public service and a great many people quite prepared to be candidates for Parliament, but we were pretty short on people who had real determination to create business activity in Canada that would extend beyond a very localized focus."

Bryden wanted to become a capitalist. The main obstacle to this desire was an absence of capital. He turned to the tested solution of the escaped bureaucrat. In other capitals, they become lobbyists, but in Ottawa there is no such thing. In fact, the word is heard only in the phrase, "I am not a lobbyist." Bryden became a consultant. "What I had was a very considerable amount of energy and quite a lot of experience in management and in the workings of government. So I set up a consulting business for the purpose of selling my knowledge." Bryden's firm was a partnership with a friend who was already a successful consulting engineer. First-year profits, after salaries, were $100,000. He now had the capital. All he needed was the opportunity. Like most, it came by chance.

Georgia Bryden is a rider and stabled her horse near Kanata, where the Brydens lived. "There was no high tech in Kanata then," Bryden recalls. "We looked out our window at where Mitel is now and all we saw was cow pasture." Another equestrian who boarded her steed at the stable was Carolyn Davies, and the two women became friends. Soon, in one of the serendipitous social encounters that ignite so many business successes, the two husbands were introduced. Carolyn's mate was computer software specialist John Davies.

After stints as a salesman for IBM and a partner in a small Ottawa computer consulting firm, Jack, as he prefers to be called, had in 1968 formed a one-man company called Softwarehouse. Business boomed, and the Softwarehouse payroll roster grew in three years to twenty-three employees, pulling in half a million dollars a year in contracts. The company was being managed by John Kelly, who later founded NABU. Davies's strength was as much in salesmanship as in software design. His natural sales talent was first revealed when, as an engineering student at Carleton University, he tried his hand at selling encyclopedias door to door. He sold ten sets in his first two weeks.

After Davies sold Softwarehouse to Systems Dimensions he remained with the bigger company to build its software division into a national network. To help develop that plan, Davies hired his acquaintance Rod Bryden to undertake a marketing study of the company's prospects in Western Canada. Bryden concluded that IBM had peppered the prairies with more hardware than anyone knew how to use. The potential for software sales was mouthwatering. But Systems Dimensions wouldn't bite, and Davies quit the company in frustration – taking along with him a band of similarly discontented and ambitious software specialists. By now, in 1974, Bryden had accumulated enough interest in the computer industry, and enough money, to join Davies's group in a fifty-fifty partnership they named Systemhouse. Davies and his five fellow defectors provided most of the expertise. Bryden supplied most of the $250,000 capital.

Prevailing industry practice was to rent out programming services by the hour. Customers simply didn't know how much a system would cost or whether it would work. The unique Systemhouse approach was to supply finished solutions – hardware, software, staff training and all – to their clients. Systemhouse offered a fixed price and a guaranteed product. As Davies and his group had wanted to do within Systems Dimensions, Systemhouse concentrated on the new so-called minicomputers, which were still the size of a refrigerator but were significantly cheaper than the big mainframes used by large corporations. Minicomputers made smaller businesses a major new market for consultants and software houses like Systemhouse.

Success came quickly. "We always got the maximum leverage out of every dollar," remembers Bryden. "In the first year we did over a million dollars worth of business on $100,000 worth of equity. The second year we did $3 million on maybe $200,000 worth of equity." During the first years, business came so easily that the company didn't even have a salesman.

The federal government, of course, was a major consumer of Systemhouse services and software. Government sales accounted for 37 per cent of the company's revenues in 1980. Bryden insists that his civil service background and Liberal Party past were more of a hindrance than an advantage because, had they known of his connection with Systemhouse, civil servants would have been leery of dealing with the company for fear of accusations of favouritism. Not only had he managed Lang's election campaign, he had also directed two failed attempts by his brother John to win the leadership of the New Brunswick Liberal Party. Worst of all, he had been the federal

Liberals' national finance chairman. All in all, a record that would bring the media and opposition hyenas howling at the scent of patronage if he were found within sight of Parliament Hill.

"Public servants and ministers are extremely reluctant to contract with people who have been at a senior level for fear of being criticized. Until April 1982, the fact that I was a large shareholder in and chairman of Systemhouse was not terribly well known. It certainly was not known around the government," Bryden says. For the first six years he virtually hid his ownership of the firm from public view. While the company carried on business on the third floor of a downtown Ottawa office building, Bryden, its chairman and chief executive officer, worked seven floors above behind doors marked "Kinburn Capital Corporation." His office looks out over the Peace Tower, the Bank of Canada, and dozens of other federal fortresses whose rooftop flutter of red and white flags makes downtown Ottawa as gaudy as a gas station in a price war.

Bryden managed to keep not only his own presence but also the entire company publicly invisible as it grew by the quiet spread of its reputation among computing specialists. "For years, unless you worked for Systemhouse or happened to have a Systemhouse employee in your office as a consultant, you probably wouldn't even have known we existed," Bryden says. "We never announced appoint-ments of executives. We never announced contracts. We never announced significant events in the company. We just didn't announce anything."

There was another motive besides the dread of conflict of interest accusations behind the Systemhouse silence. The company feared that news of its success would not be welcome in a city where business is distrusted on principle and where belief in the country's inescapable mediocrity is an ideological foundation of protectionist policies in everything from the economy through broadcasting to the arts. "Now that high tech is taking off, it's getting to be the in thing, but it used to be the case that the last thing they wanted to hear was that somebody local was successful. It simply generated jealousy and determination to be sure that those guys didn't get too much." This reaction was, Bryden believes, an expression of "a basic Canadian attitude of assuming that what is local is second rate."

Bryden accumulated an increasing share of the firm's ownership through a chain of holding companies that resulted from his various investment partnerships. His investments were grouped under a personal company called R.M. Bryden Holdings, which owned another called East Coast Investments, which in turn owned Kinburn Capital. Kinburn was the majority owner of Systemhouse. Should the paperless society fail to emerge from the computerization of information, Bryden's bets are covered by heavy investments in the technology of recycling old paper boxes into corrugated cardboard. In 1979, Kinburn diversified by acquiring control of Trent Valley Paperboard Mills in Trenton, Ontario, and then added four corrugated box companies in Toronto and Montreal.

By 1980, Systemhouse was growing so rapidly that it could not finance its expansion from profits. Its revenues were increasing by more than 50 per cent a year, but there was a steady gap of millions of dollars between its expenditures on current projects and recovery of that money from the customers once the work was done and an invoice submitted. Systemhouse paid for its growth by borrowing from the bank, using Bryden's shares in the company as collateral. As business increased, so did the value of those shares, so that by the time the company decided to offer stock to the public, Bryden's stake in Systemhouse was calculated at about $2 million and his ownership at 65 per cent.

Bryden began to emerge teasingly from his anonymity about the time that Systemhouse decided to invite public investment. His background in management and finance would be perceived to be a reassuring complement to Davies's knowledge of software and sales. Besides, financial analysts and potential investors had a right to know who was running the company.

The transition of Systemhouse from privately owned to publicly traded company coincided with the company's decision to develop packaged software, programs that are designed to work for more than one company in the same industry. Previously, computer programs had been written for each client the way a house builder would work from the original and unique design of an architect. The expense of this procedure effectively denied the benefits of computerization to hundreds of businesses that could afford the machines, which were getting cheaper, but not the custom software, which was getting more expensive. The alternative to making software that would fit the user's way of doing business was to get the user to adapt his business practices to a standard piece of software.

Packaged software can be sold for perhaps 5 per cent of its development cost, a saving that might justify modification of a firm's old clerical habits. The added annoyance could even be beneficial. Packaged software is written to conform to the standard practices of the particular industry it is designed to serve, adoption of which probably will improve the operations of most potential buyers. The packaged programs can, if necessary, be fiddled with to take account of a customer's idiosyncrasies and still cost substantially less than a whole set of programs written from scratch. The Systemhouse financial management package for distribution companies, which does financial applications, general ledgers, and inventory control, cost about $3 million to write, test, and debug. It is sold for $30,000 a copy. "There are thousands of customers that can afford to pay $30,000," notes Bryden. "but damn few that can afford to pay $3 million."

With the advent of packaged software, programming houses could no longer depend for their living on hard work and a fairly quick return on time invested in writing a software system for a single client. The reward for a software package that is sold for a small fraction of its development cost is ultimately greater, but much longer in coming. Greater capital is needed to pay the programmers to make products that earn nothing before they are completed and then cost still more to market. Banks do not clamour to finance such ventures. But the possibility of rewards commensurate with the high risk does draw the interest of private investors.

The first public offering of Systemhouse stock netted $2,750,000. Systemhouse employees themselves bought $250,000 worth of that stock and Bryden purchased $500,000 worth. A few months later the company went back with a second issue that fattened its capital by $23 million. Systemhouse used the money, as it had promised, to develop software packages and to set up a marketing network to sell them throughout North America. But public companies have a responsibility to report their activities to shareholders, and with the firm's new public profile controversy once more lay in wait for Rod Bryden.

Systemhouse was spending vast amounts of money developing software with the expectation of return to come in succeeding years, just as a mining company spends millions digging a pit before it can sell ore. Mining companies report the cost of digging the hole as an asset because it is a capital expense incurred to generate revenue. Bryden did the same with the cost of developing new software. It became, in Bryden's own description, "an extremely controversial application of accounting practice. If we put $3 million into a new office building, we'd carry it on our balance sheet. And if we put $3 million into a new software package, then we'd put that on our balance sheet. We'll indicate what it is, and depreciate it at the appropriate rate, and expect to make money from it. In the event we don't, the depreciation will be a drag on earnings in the same way as if you put your money into an office building where the rental is not as high as you hoped it was going to be: the depreciation and interest costs would be a drag on your earnings. Exactly the same. Nothing magical about it at all. The only people who have any trouble with that are financial analysts. They seem to believe that because an asset is intangible it therefore is not real, and that for us to carry on our balance sheet the asset that investors expected us to buy with the money they gave us is somehow not ethically right. I think that is patently absurd."

Bryden reluctantly, and without admitting error, compromised to reassure investors worried by the tut-tuts of the analysts and the accountants. Now, money spent on new programs is counted as an asset only to an amount equal to the drop in book value of other, established programs. The rest of the development money is reported as an expense. "The analysts will think that's very responsible and the chartered accountants will feel very happy and relieved about it. The public, however, may be misled because it will believe the company made less money than it did and that it has fewer assets than it actually has," Bryden complains.

What really called attention to Systemhouse's accounting methods in its nasty year of 1982 was the evaporation of its new investors' capital. A lot of it was lost because of extravagantly ambitious planning. Millions were spent on a network of sales offices throughout the United States manned with a layer of regional managers who would be required to co-ordinate the anticipated rush of new orders. The computer business seemed to be healthy, Systemhouse had proven programs to sell, and the company waited for the profits to pour in, driving up the price of the stock and providing yet more funds for program development. Then, nothing happened. The cake was made, the streamers were hung, but nobody came to the party.

"What is so unusual about the software industry," Bryden explains, "is that it is not unusual." He compares the branch expansion to the installation of a new paper machine in his Trenton mill. "In the year when you turn on the new machine, sales have got to pop up." Unfortunately for Systemhouse, just at the moment it turned on its $29-million sales machine, recession hit North America. Demand for computer programs dropped along with everything else. But System-house took a little longer than most others to realize it. Blithely considering itself to be immune to recession, Systemhouse carried on hiring new staff right through to March 1982 at salaries ranging from $21,000 for young programmers without experience to near $50,000 for senior consultants. The company's zooming expansion from a staff of 574 employees when it went public in 1980 to 1,067 eighteen months later destroyed the intimate internal relationships that had been part of its collegial management style and replaced them with confusion. And because of the company's management tradition and the nature of computer professionals generally, it was hard to impose shifts in direction.

There is little cultural or class distinction between a starting pro-grammer and the company president, Bryden notes. Because machines do all the dirty work, the software industry does not have a blue-collar work force. Bryden discovered that "people are less willing to accept direction when they have every reason to believe, probably accurately, that their own judgement is every bit as good as that of the guy in authority. Structured management is more easily imple-mented in an organization where there tends to be greater faith in executives because there is a greater disparity in knowledge and self-confidence between the executive and those they are trying to lead. The less the disparity, the less automatic the authority chain and the more it is necessary to explain why every single step is taken. To some degree that imposes constraints on structured management and costs in the operation of a business."

By April 1982, Systemhouse was losing $3 million a month. Bryden's discreet supervision of the company suddenly turned visible and aggressive. "I came a little farther out of the closet because it was apparent that there was a need for very urgent action," he says. "Things had to be done right away, things which were totally at odds with the whole history of our growth, a whole lot of things that are not a whole lot of fun to do." Bryden decided to take full personal command. He assumed Davies's title of president while keeping his own of chairman and chief executive officer. Davies moved to Fairfax, Virginia, to take charge of a pared down U.S. marketing operation, and in August 1983 would leave Systemhouse altogether.

Investor confidence in Bryden's ability to save his company was so low that Systemhouse stock, which had been worth $3.25 when first issued in August 1980 and in its heyday had hit $13.00, plummeted to 85 cents. Bryden cut back the Systemhouse staff from 1,067 to 715; he closed three offices and all the regional headquarters of the U.S. sales network. Systemhouse was taking a breather, depending on its existing catalogue of proven programs to generate enough return to restore the trust of the stock market.

As it regained its balance, Systemhouse was pondering an entry into the hardware side of the computer business. A product that Systemhouse called the personal work station had first been installed in the Department of National Defence under a federal program to stimulate Canadian companies to develop advanced office systems. As the company contemplated mass distribution of the terminal to business customers, even Rod Bryden was getting ready to put one of the things on his own desk, although he wasn't quite clear as to just what it would do. "It's a troublesome damn thing to try to describe exactly. It's a work station for a non-clerical officer or worker in the company, not just an executive."

Systemhouse survived, chastened, and with a leaner, better-structured management cured of the intoxication of growth. The experience cost Bryden some of his pride, and more of his equity in the company. To keep it alive, he had to inject another $14 million, part of which was equity and part borrowed from banks on the collateral of his investments in cardboard boxes. Another $4 million was invested by Bytec after Bryden appealed personally to Michael Cowpland. Bytec also gained a seat for Glen St. John on the Systemhouse board and an option to buy more stock later. Systemhouse sought new capital from its existing shareholders through an issue of attractively priced shares. If Bytec and the other shareholders exercise their rights to buy, Bryden's share of the company will be reduced to 30 per cent with Bytec holding 18 per cent.

Bryden's challenge now is to expand sales while rebuilding his company's research and development capacity. Software is not only an intangible commodity but one that perishes as competitors match or surpass it. Systemhouse cannot rely for long on its assets of proven programs and must soon find funds to pay for the renewal of research. In this regard, he says, "I would much prefer to finance research and development from the marketplace. But to the extent that the financial analysts and the accounting profession force the industry to treat investments in technological assets as though they were of no value, the ability to get financing to make those investments will be impaired."

The only alternative, he laments, is government money, in one form or another. And that is why, despite his sarcasm about Sydney Development being a river for people who would rather throw money away than pay taxes, Systemhouse too applied for an advanced tax ruling in 1982 with which it hoped to pay for the development of new software. But in the darkest of the company's days it fell victim to the rebels in the revenue department and their moratorium on advance tax rulings. Though the whole fight escaped the notice of the daily news media, a true power struggle was under way between civil servants and elected politicians, one that went beyond mere tax issues to the very question of who has constitutional authority to run the country.

The mutinous tax collectors had tasted the joys of illicit power in the disastrous 1981 budget of Allan MacEachen, then finance minister, who carelessly gave free rein to officials determined to impose their own standards of equity. The politicians, in their opinion, had gone soft on capitalism. The favourable ruling issued in 1981 to Tarrnie Williams's Sydney Development Corporation and Northern's use of the R&D tax shelter to pass on large attractive tax savings to corporate investors worried the faceless gnomes within the revenue department. But what really offended their pride was a brochure that the Ministry of State for Science and Technology distributed to high-tech firms setting out exactly how they could create tax shelters to finance research and development. Both the principle of the tax shelter and the intrusion of another ministry into their affairs piqued the revenue officials. Senior bureaucrats of both departments shouted abuse at each other over the phone and in face-to-face meetings.

At the time, William Hutchison was president of the Canadian Advanced Technology Association, which favoured the tax shelters for its members. The revenue department is "a group unto itself," according to Hutchison, whose role as spokesman for Canadian-owned electronics firms involved him in the mess. "The revenue officials view themselves as separate from the rest of the world. Somebody needs to bring them in line and tell them they are part of the government."

Cabinet ministers gave Bryden personal assurances that the revenue revolt would be crushed and that advance tax rulings would be issued. But the ruling never came, and Bryden was forced to fire a hundred people whose salaries would have been financed by the tax shelter offering. The tax shelter dispute was finally resolved late in 1982, too late for all but a handful of high-tech companies to make use of it. Ironically, one of the first favourable advance tax rulings that signalled the end of the moratorium was issued to Sydney Development, which quickly used it to raise another $6.63 million from investors seeking shelter from taxes.

The government won, but not before dumping the minister. Like a unit of the Spanish Guardia Civil too powerful to punish for attempting to topple a parliament, the insurgents still lurk within the revenue department.

"If somebody in my company upon receiving a direction said, 'Up yours,' he'd be looking for a job, like right now," says Bryden bitterly. "The government didn't do that. Instead, it changed the minister." Bryden concedes the civil servant's duty to resist undue political interference. But in this case he insists – and just about everybody else involved agrees – that the will of Parliament was being flouted by a bunch of renegade bureaucrats on the wrong side of the law. "I used to teach tax law. They were absolutely, categorically, for sure, definitely wrong in the department. If Systemhouse had been in better financial shape and I didn't have to turn my attention to something else, the outcome of that might have been somewhat different. And it may yet be. I have a short list of things to do after I get the world in order internally. Some individuals who were not helpful when the world was difficult may have thought that I didn't notice or was unable to respond. Neither was true."

Bryden pauses long and hard before deciding whether his roller-coaster ride has been fun. "Fun is skiing. I like skiing and I like playing tennis and I enjoy swimming, golf. I enjoy my farm in New Brunswick and I enjoy my granddaughter. That's all fun. I would not call the business fun. But as work, I wouldn't want to have worked at anything different. If I were to rewrite the last ten years, I wouldn't change them much. I wouldn't have the stock drop to eighty-five cents and I think brinkmanship is an enjoyable part of business only so long as it doesn't occur too often. For a little while last year we had too many situations that were too close to the brink."

CHAPTER EIGHT

The Sorceror's Apprentice

Roderick Bryden gratefully acknowledges that Systemhouse would have tumbled over the brink into oblivion if it hadn't been for Michael Cowpland's $4-million bailout. "Mike made a lot of money in high tech and he understands there can be setbacks," Bryden says. "His wasn't the major part of the money, but it was the crucial part."

Cowpland himself professes dismay at being placed upon a pedestal as some sort of deity of Canadian high tech but the fact is that his free-wheeling drive to the top has made him a model of ambition and accomplishment for aspiring engineer-entrepreneurs. His wealth has also made him an attractive financial patron to conceivers of exciting new black boxes without the resources to make them into commercial products.

Murray Bell says he always used to think of Mike Cowpland as a god. Cowpland did, long before high-tech entrepreneurs had become folk heroes of the new age, what Bell had wanted to do himself: make a world success of a Canadian high-tech enterprise. Now, with Cowpland's help, Bell can claim to have achieved that aim, and has perhaps become a multimillionaire in the process. But he's not happy about the experience or satisfied by the results. Instead, Bell is back where he started from, still as obsessed as ever with the quest for the right black box, and determined this time to avoid going to Cowpland or anyone else for help. If Cowpland is a god, then, to Murray Bell, he is a capricious god.

Now in his late thirties and under the threat of paunch, which he fights on the racquetball court, Bell speaks softly and has an expression that seems gentle and friendly compared to the lean hungry look that characterizes many other engineers who have succeeded as businessmen. He is more studious than most of them and doggedly consumes computer industry research reports and newsletters for intelligence about market developments and opportunities for new business ventures. He is also a compulsive tinkerer who has to have some new mechanical toy to play with.

Bell was one of those nomadic children of the military who knew where they were born but couldn't really say where they came from. His Air Force dad took the family along from one base to another, a way of life that produced either gregarious youngsters, quick to work their way into new gangs, or shy, withdrawn ones like Murray Bell, who discovered his satisfactions in personal projects. "When I was about ten years old on the Portage la Prairie base out in Manitoba I saved my money – about twenty or thirty dollars, which was a lot for me then – and sent away for this kit which purported to be a digital computer," he muses. "It was sort of a peg board with a bunch of disks, and you made up your own switches. If you were very patient, you could design a sort of switching circuit and it became, in a sense, a computer. It was a sort of mechanical analog of a digital computer."

Murray also built a robot with his Meccano set, powered it with a couple of electric motors, and sent it off across the floor, arms flapping and eyes alight. This, his parents thought, was creativity to be encouraged, certainly more than their son's experiments in chemistry. "I built rockets with sulphur and zinc. I guess I was a mad scientist kind of kid. I was usually at the top of the class. I had time to do those things," he says now. He was an Ontario Scholar at his high school graduation in Ottawa. His father, like many military officers, became a recruiter and pushed Murray to apply for entry to the Regular Officer Training Plan. The military offered sixteen-year-old youths, not considered in other circumstances to be legally responsible for commitments of such magnitude, a paid university education in return for three years of active service after graduation. "I wasn't particularly inclined to do it, but I went for the tests and interviews. I got accepted by the Air Force, but I really didn't want to go to Royal Military College so I applied to go to Queen's instead, where there was an ROTP squadron which met once a week."

Queen's University and Kingston, Ontario, in the 1960s were the scene of Bell's social coming out, an awakening that would see him transformed from a shy child to a man of open warmth whose enthusiasm and honest innocence have survived undamaged from childhood. If he suffers from a social fault it's that his trust in others makes him so obviously vulnerable to betrayal which in turn arouses an uncomfortable protectiveness in those around him. He's simply a nice guy, a brilliant engineer who once had to drive himself to ruthlessness to save his machine.

Bell studied engineering physics at Queen's and at the end of his four years won the Governor General's Medal for the highest class standing. "I made a lot friends at Queen's. The reason, I think, is that we had come from all over the country and were all strangers to one another. It was much easier to break in and make friends than it was travelling around with the armed forces."

Now the Air Force summoned him to move again, to serve his three years as an officer. Again Bell was reluctant. "I was really interested in engineering physics and electrical engineering, and I applied to several graduate schools with the idea of asking for a leave of absence to get a higher degree." He was offered a fellowship by Massachusetts Institute of Technology and, with the blessing of the military, went to Boston for a year to earn his Master's in electrical engineering with a thesis on atomic clocks.

By then the call of the military could no longer be ignored, and Bell was assigned a desk in Ottawa as a project officer for the Directorate of Aerospace Combat Systems. It was, as it turned out, just a fancy government name for boredom. As he describes it, "I worked on armaments for fighter aircraft. I was actually working on studies for the F-18. It took ten years for that thing to happen. I worked on all sorts of things – guided missiles, rockets, that sort of stuff. But it was basically a paperwork exercise, not very exciting. It was kind of fun, though, because it was a nine-to-five job, and I learned to ski and actually got married at that time. So it's probably just as well."

In May 1970, Bell's debt to Her Majesty was cleared and he got out of the service, content to stay in Ottawa but in a hurry to get back to engineering. "I looked up computers in the Yellow Pages. There was this company called Consolidated Computer and I found out that they were working with a Digital Equipment minicomputer, not the really big things but something you could get your hands around."

Consolidated Computer was then, before its eventual bankruptcy,

167

intensely committed to its ultimately successful key edit system. The key edit system bypassed the process of feeding information to computers with paper cards punched through with precise, rectangular holes by armies of women pounding away at keyboards. Bell joined the development group and eventually became project manager of a team of eight engineers and technologists. "Some of the guys I hired there ended up as vice-presidents at Mitel. It's interesting to watch these things spin off into other companies in the area."

Bell himself was getting ready to spin off but needed to learn more, both about computers and about business. Eighteen months after his arrival at Consolidated, the company went into receivership, and Bell went across the Ottawa River to the dingy industrial town of Hull, Quebec, where the Canadian subsidiary of Data General Corporation was making Nova minicomputers, a precursor of the Eagle, which author Tracy Kidder would make famous in his 1982 Pulitzer Prize winning book, *The Soul of a New Machine*. Data General needed someone to take charge of designing special interfaces, made-to-measure connections of computers to a customer's own equipment and instruments. One of Bell's big jobs for Data General was linking the Nova to a brain scanner at Sherbrooke General Hospital in the Eastern Townships of Quebec.

A year and a half later, in 1973, Bell figured he was ready, and he quit Data General. Bell's wife, Carol, recalls that there was nothing spontaneous about her husband's decision. "It's something he always wanted to do. The first time I ever met him he said he wanted to start a high-technology company in Canada." Bell himself recollects, "I'd been looking for the right opportunity, the right product with which to start a company, and the floppy disk seemed to be the right one."

The floppy disk had been invented by IBM to feed programs to their big mainframe computers. It is essentially a magnetic ring containing its information in concentric tracks, much like a phonograph record. The smaller minicomputers at that time still depended on either paper tape punched with holes or reels of magnetic tape. A U.S. company had just revealed a machine that would read floppy disks and feed their information to the smaller computers, and Bell thought that he could improve upon the idea.

He began tinkering in the basement of his Ottawa split-level and soldered together a thing called a controller, which allowed the drives that read the floppy disks to talk to the minicomputer. His enthusiasm for the new technology infected an itinerant salesman, Gary Davis, who had been calling regularly at Data General to sell printers and other computer peripherals to Bell's special projects group. Davis recruited his own boss to the venture and, each partner laying down his five-thousand-dollar entrepreneur's dues, they created Dynalogic Corporation. Operations were then moved from Bell's basement to a tiny room in a building that later became a Pop Shoppe soft-drink store. "I went out and bought a Nova from a used computer company in the States," Bells recalls. "About April, I got it working with the disk drive."

Bell's salesman-partner performed too, coming up with a potential buyer in Toronto – the McBee Company, which was selling an accounting system that relied on punched paper tape to feed a rather passé Litton computer. Bell winces still, ten years later. "It was ancient, archaic, and I told Gary I couldn't design anything for that piece of junk." But Davis responded with wisdom Bell would have to live with as a businessman: "Look, it's a customer."

Bell worked through the summer to make the interface that would let his floppy disks communicate with that "horrible machine." He toiled until 3 a.m. the day of the delivery deadline, put his machine into the trunk of his car, and drove through the dawn from Ottawa to Toronto. After six months in business, Dynalogic had netted a profit of $311.

This was meagre compensation for Carol Bell who, with a young baby, rarely saw her husband. "I don't think entrepreneurs are so wonderful. There were a lot of all-nighters at the beginning. Murray found it exciting, but it was difficult for the family. He did work a lot of necessary hours in the initial years. But then, I think, it became a habit. It became strange not to work strange hours." Her husband, she says, is depressed by calm routine. He comes alive only when another scheme hijacks his mind and sends him off once again in pursuit of a success. "Money's not the motive," Carol says. "It's something driving him from within."

Bell, ten years after quitting his job to found Dynalogic, recognizes the obsessive pattern of his career as an entrepreneur. "My wife will tell you, I'm always promising that I just have to work a little harder on this project and it's going to be the big winner. I guess she's probably heard that story no less than a dozen times. So now she just smiles and says, 'Yes, Murray.'"

Bell's floppy disk gizmo worked, and twenty more were ordered by the McBee Company, then another fifty, and another fifty after that at four thousand dollars each. Dynalogic now actually had term deposits in a bank account. Word of the floppy disk success was spreading, and Monroe Calculator Company asked Bell to link disks to one of its powerful desktop calculators. "Again, it was kind of a weird interface, but that's probably why we got the business," Bell says. Monroe eventually bought fifty or so of the units to resell to its Canadian customers, and the company's U.S. parent looked at but didn't buy the Dynalogic system. The American company then started making its own disk units, and Bell feels that his design had been copied. Dynalogic lost Monroe's business altogether when the Canadian subsidiary began buying the drives from its American parent, and thus Dynalogic was suddenly abandoned by its only significant customer.

Bell had hoped to sell some of his floppy disk systems to CNCP Telecommunications for a national police information network CNCP was setting up. Dynalogic's disks would have been used in local police headquarters to store crime data retrieved over CNCP's lines connected to a central cop computer in Ottawa. But negotiations faltered and it appeared that the deal was off. Prospects for the company were bleak.

A $75,000 venture capital loan from the Ontario government briefly stayed Dynalogic's dissolution in 1976, but when that ran out it appeared inevitable that the eight employees would have to go and bankruptcy proceedings would begin. Bell and his partners got together one Friday and told themselves that it was all over. It was at 4:30 that afternoon that CNCP phoned to order the disk systems. Over the next three years, CNCP bought five hundred Dynalogic disk units and some of the several million dollars in steady revenue this business brought was spent by Bell's little company in the design of an advanced microcomputer.

In 1976, while Steve Jobs and Steve Wozniak were putting together the first Apples in a California garage, Dynalogic was building its own similar machine. But Bell equipped his microcomputer with powers and components surpassing the standards of the nascent industry.

He was then unaware of an unfortunate truth about technological evolutions: the first system that works most of the time becomes a standard that both sellers and buyers will stick to.

Dynalogic sold some of its microcomputers, but because they were designed with emphasis on engineering, instead of marketing, principles, the machines were not the commercial success they might have been if they had been technologically just a bit less advanced. "You've got to be aware of those de facto standards and how important they are to the acceptability of your product – something I didn't understand back then," Bell comments ruefully.

Because of its unique central nervous system, Dynalogic's microcomputer could run only its own software and was cut off from the growing library of programs being written for the software system called CP/M, generally accepted as a standard by the industry and consumers. Bell and his programmers opted instead for a superior but then more obscure system called UNIX, which came into its own only in the early 1980s as microcomputers began to be linked together in networks that share common printers and storage devices. Still, only an engineer lost in the esoterica of his art could, like Bell, toss off a phrase like "before UNIX was the household word it is now."

More than three hundred Dynalogic microcomputers were sold, some of them in Great Britain, Belgium, France, and Germany. By 1979, the company was touching $1 million in annual sales of its computer and floppy disk systems, but, Bell admits, "we never sold enough of any one thing to get that critical mass which you need to really grow as a company. We based our marketing decisions on what just one or two customers would say, which is very dangerous. We'd design these products and they'd all work fine, but we couldn't sell very many of them."

Dynalogic's momentum was failing, and with the onset of the recession in 1981, Bell knew the company would need more capital to pursue the quest for that one product that would carry it over the threshold between struggling start-up firm and and established company. In the spring of that year, when Dynalogic's finances were getting tight, Bell's bank manager suggested that he talk to another of the bank's clients, Glen St. John, president of Michael Cowpland's Bytec Management. St. John and Cowpland were impressed by

Dynalogic's engineering talent and purchased an 80-per-cent share of the company from Bell. The cash he received was just enough to pay off Dynalogic's debts.

Bell's experience as an entrepreneur had so far been less than financially rewarding; indeed, his wife points out, he could have made a lot more money working as a salaried engineer. Now, with the financial strength of Bytec behind him, Bell seemed to be enjoying the best of both worlds, with the salary of a company president and the resources to create a winning product that would still be recognized as his. For a brief period, Bytec tried to mate high tech and the hewing of wood by merging its furniture-making subsidiary, Kombi, and Dynalogic. But an attempt to build microelectronic communications systems into the desk top didn't work, largely because the electronics engineers and the cabinetmakers just couldn't get along professionally or personally. The marriage was annulled, and later, in February 1983, after losing $6 million in five years, Kombi and its bankers called in a receiver.

There remained after the dissolution of that merger the problem of finding something for Dynalogic to do. The idea for the machine that would satisfy the need was truly a joint inspiration. St. John suggested a portable microcomputer along the lines of the popular and inexpensive Osborne, made in California. Cowpland was more intrigued by the thought of a portable electronic mail terminal, which travelling businessmen could connect to their hotel telephones to exchange written messages with their home offices. Bell said both a portable computer and an electronic mail terminal could be combined in the same machine. Because of his disappointing experience with Dynalogic's earlier microcomputer, which required a unique set of programs, Bell insisted that the machine run a standard and commonly available class of software. IBM had just released its elegant Personal Computer. It had instantly become an acquisition of prestige, and Bell predicted, quite correctly, that the IBM machine would quickly take its place as a new industry standard and that a plentiful supply of software would follow. IBM's computer really added little to the technology of the little machines except a high degree of quality and, above all, the reassuring IBM logo. Most of its innards were in fact not made by IBM at all and could be found in the machines of many competitors.

172

Over Christmas 1981, Bell and his thirty-one-year-old engineering manager, Paul Barsley, drew up the specifications for their dream machine. Barsley was a veteran of the contingent of immigrant British engineers that landed at Bell-Northern Research. He had been deeply involved in designing Northern's Displayphone, and a senior Northern executive would later note that the Dynalogic computer's communications and electronic mail system was probably better than Displayphone's. Bell-Northern follows the progress of its departed employees with a parent's confused sentiments of pride and loss.

In early January, Bell and Barsley presented their plans to Cowpland and St. John. The Bytec executives liked them, gave Bell the go-ahead and a project group was organized into a new Bytec subsidiary called Dynalogic Info-Tech. Bytec would hold 83 per cent of it. Bell and Dynalogic's other original shareholders held the rest, with the possibility of doubling their equity a year later if the product was successfully developed by then.

Bell was now in his element, having an exciting engineering project, an impossible deadline, and all the money he needed for the job. Working from offices and laboratories divided between two buildings in industrial parkland south of Ottawa, the engineers pulled together the parts of the machine they wanted to make.

The most brilliant design stroke had nothing to do with electronics. Bell's machine was built with an engineer's indulgence in excellence but this time with one eye on the marketplace. Such a superlative machine was bound to be expensive, and that meant it must be a prestige product fit for a CEO's credenza. The operative word among the Dynalogic designers was "sexy." Appearance would count as much as performance, and Cowpland told Bell to ask a California consultant named David Kelly to undertake the moulding of the computer's case. It was Kelly who had shaped the plastic shells of Apple's machines, including its newest, the Lisa.

Kelly accepted the project and showed Bell and Barsley a first mockup made of styrofoam. Then, working together, they made a second model of cardboard and paper, using felt-tip markers to ink in the screen area, control buttons, and slits for the disk drives. The result was stunning in its logical simplicity. Its colouring would be an unashamed imitation of IBM's two-tone cream and clay. A few hand-crafted cases were glued together by a model maker in Palo Alto while the engineers continued to shuffle chips about the circuit boards, figuring out how they were going to stuff that much power into such a little box.

Bell decided, early in the spring of 1982, that things were going well and that he should divulge the machine's existence as soon as possible to attract distributors and gain the advantage of the attention that the first IBM-compatible portable microcomputer would inevitably attract. The second one would be greeted as just another copy. Twice each year there is a huge U.S. computer trade show called Comdex. Bell decided to stage the machine's début at the 1982 spring Comdex in Atlantic City.

Dynalogic hired Taylor-Sprules Corporation to produce the brochures, booklets, and posters for the June unveiling. The resulting high gloss seared the eyes like the sunshine reflected by a snow-covered lake. The machine was pictured floating on a cloud. The text was categorical: "The Most Powerful, Portable, Business Computer in the World." Even while the blurbs were being written, the machine was still without a name. "Passport" and "Blue Chip" were in the running, but the winner was "Hyperion," the name of the Greek Titan who was father of the Sun, the Moon, and Aurora, goddess of the dawn. The name was chosen just weeks before the Atlantic City show. The name, the promotional brochures, and the planning of the machine's introduction cost Dynalogic $300,000. Development of the machine itself consumed less than $1 million.

The brochures, however, were ready before the machine was. The Friday before the Monday show opening in Atlantic City, Hyperion was still a comatose collection of chips and circuit boards. Once more Bell and his engineers worked through the night, breathing life into the first two prototypes. The next day, he rented a Lear jet, strapped in his precious computers, and flew the design team south to share in the acceptance or rejection of this shy new kid on a tough block where it was hard to make friends or stake out new territory.

The only living Hyperions turned out to be the darlings of Atlantic City, their demo program of text and a graphic map of the United States glowing warmly in amber – a colour common among European computers but then unique in North America, where monochrome screens were either white or green on black. Its built-in ability to communicate with other computers over the phone lines was also raved about in the industry press.

The U.S. bi-weekly *Electronics* reported that "Canada dropped a 20-pound bombshell on Atlantic City." Bell returned home more excited than ever about his project but well aware that it still wasn't performing the way the brochures promised. He also would have to learn to manage a manufacturing and marketing operation far beyond anything in his experience. He realized that his entrepreneurial style of leadership, in which he involved himself in the tiniest details of design and organization, would have to give way to the delegation of control to professional managers. Bell had already hired a vice-president of marketing, and in August he hired William Lipski to take charge of manufacturing. Lipski had been a director of manufacturing at Northern Telecom.

Wanting to become a hard-nosed manager as well as a skilled engineer, Bell went to Jasper Lodge to attend the American Management Association's annual summer course for company presidents. "I was determined to be a president who could grow with his company." The presidents used their own firms as case studies, and Bell described Dynalogic's lack of distribution channels for a product that would soon go into manufacture. "Being an engineer, I had never really been exposed to a lot of the complicated and sophisticated marketing things. How do you handle market research, ad placement, dealer contracts, those kinds of things." Bell's vice-president for marketing didn't seem to know either, and this was the problem Bell put to his fellow presidents. They were unanimous. He would have to get rid of his marketing man and hire a new one or risk the disintegration of his enterprise.

Resolving to be tougher than the dictates of his own personality, Bell went home and fired his vice-president. He was now convinced that Dynalogic's urgent priority must be the hiring of a hot-shot marketing strategist. "I'd pay him $100,000 plus a few stock options. It would be worth it. A guarantee that you're going to be successful. What we needed was somebody who sold for Apple or one of the biggies. Maybe I was overreacting because of my past experience, but I felt pretty strongly that that was the area where we were really weak."

So Bell began what turned into a campaign to get permission from Cowpland and St. John in Bytec to hire a marketing star. Meanwhile, the partners who controlled Ontario's important ComputerLand franchise wanted to see the Hyperion perform. They brought along disks from their IBM Personal Computer to verify that the Hyperion was indeed compatible. Unfortunately, none of them would work with the Dynalogic machine, and the ComputerLand executives returned to Toronto shaking their heads at the gap between the Hyperion publicity and its actual performance. Without IBM-compatibility, the Hyperion would be a dud in the marketplace.

The computer had to be modified and, after having been brought out with such great fanfare in Atlantic City, it also had to be delivered. In October, Dynalogic moved into its new building on the southern fringe of Ottawa. Like most high-tech plants, it was more office than factory. The assembly area consisted of rows of work tables where a terrifyingly small group of people slipped the pieces into their proper slots. It illustrated further what a brief walk through any microelectronics factory makes evident to anybody, except desperate politicians: the computer industry will not generate manufacturing jobs. Increasingly, computer assembly is being concentrated in specialist companies where other computers and robots do most of the work.

Four months after the Hyperion's unveiling, production had not yet started, and even the two original prototypes had been dissected and no longer existed. The Canadian Computer Show in Toronto and the fall Comdex show in Las Vegas were both approaching, and Dynalogic would hardly survive the humiliation of being unable to display production units by then. Cowpland and St. John were starting to worry about both the amount of money Bytec had already sunk into the project – more than $3 million in equity and loan guarantees – and the nagging problem of whether the Hyperion could be made compatible with IBM programs. Since the computer still didn't really exist, it was hard for Bell to allay Bytec's concerns on either score.

Cowpland began checking personally on the Hyperion's progress, arriving late in the day at the plant, often with his friend Ross Tuddenham. At the same time, Cowpland didn't want his preoccupation with Bytec to become too obvious, fearing that Mitel investors would loose confidence in his attention to that bigger, more mature company, which was having problems of its own with the SX-2000 telephone exchange. So Cowpland kept his meetings with St. John discreet. "We did a lot of business on the tennis and the racquetball court, and we had the occasional breakfast meeting," he says. Cowpland also delegated some of his worries about the Hyperion to Tuddenham, who began using a big office in the front corner of the Dynalogic building as his own, though he had no official status in either Bytec or Dynalogic. "His mandate was to go in there and have a look at what was wrong with the marketing," Cowpland said months later.

Bell did not seem to sense the coming storm as he concentrated on the Hyperion's hardware and the bigger task of making it accept software written for IBM's microcomputer. He worried more than he should have about the positioning of rubber pads to keep the keyboard from sliding on desk tops and the appearance of the cardboard box the computer would be shipped in.

If Bell had been less a meticulous engineer and more a corporate politician, he would have been aware sooner of the manoeuvring above him. Cowpland had raised the possibility of merging Dynalogic into Bytec as a division, but Bell dismissed it as just a passing thought thrown out for discussion.

Bell made it to the Toronto computer show in November after yet another last-minute dash, this time to Michigan to pick up the first not-quite-finished plastic cases from their injection mould. The cases had to be spray painted to give them their pebble finish. Two weeks later the Las Vegas Comdex show opened, and by then there were a dozen very real Hyperions to exhibit at Dynalogic's booth and even to lend to software producers who were there to display their IBM programs. Dynalogic's booth was mobbed by computer stores and independent distributors wanting to take it on. But what the Hyperion really needed, as much for reasons of credibility as of distribution, was a decision by one of the big U.S. chains to make room for it on already crowded shelves. California's ComputerLand would have been the biggest capture, but without the endorsement of Canadian ComputerLand stores, this was just about impossible.

A few days after the Las Vegas show, Dynalogic received its first substantial order. A chain of ten retail stores based in Boston ordered a thousand Hyperions for delivery in 1983. That would mean

$3 million in revenue for Dynalogic. (Dynalogic's factory price to retailers was half its $5,000 U.S. retail price.) Each unit would cost two thousand American dollars to make and package. Direct labour costs per machine were only $150. At the planned peak production of four hundred units per week, only ninety-two plant workers would be needed.

It was the intention from the start that if the Hyperion were to take off in the United States, manufacturing would have to be contracted in that country to one of the big assembly firms. Because it was anticipated that 80 per cent of sales would be in the United States, concentration of manufacturing in Canada would mean components would have to be moved across the border twice with useless and time-consuming paperwork every time parts and computers came within the bureaucratic range of customs officials. Dynalogic asked SCI Systems of Huntsville, Alabama, which made the circuit boards of IBM's PC, to submit a bid for the mass manufacture of the Hyperion, from circuit boards to packaging. Dynalogic's Ottawa plant would be, in Bell's term, "the knowledge centre."

Seeing the machine finally in production and the intense interest of independent distributors in the United States, Bytec's executives seemed to gain confidence in the product but were growing frustrated with Bell, who kept harping away at the need to hire a hot-shot marketing specialist. "I thought our window was closing very quickly," Bell says. "We had the product, but it takes much more than that today to be successful. Marketing. A good product is only the entry fee to the starting gate. You have to run the race with everybody else, including the big guys." Cowpland, St. John, and the man with no title or clear authority, Tuddenham, kept their intentions to themselves.

Generally speaking, the Hyperion's prospects were good. Bell travelled to California in early December 1982 and made two big sales, one for five thousand Hyperions to computer supplier Anderson Jacobson that would distribute the machine to its business clients and another for five hundred to an engineering firm. Upon his return, satisfied with the sales and the progress the engineers were making in tying up the technical loose ends, Bell thought that this time unequivocal success was at last within his grasp. Then, on Monday, December 13, Bell had an unexpected visitor: Ross Tuddenham.

178

Tuddenham was brusque. He handed Bell a sheet of typed paper and demanded that he sign it. "I thought I was being fired," Bell said a few days later. The letter was Bell's consent to a corporate reorganization. He would become chairman of Dynalogic and Glen St. John would take over, with the real power, as president. Tuddenham was clearly acting as Cowpland's agent, and there was little to be gained by resisting. Bell signed.

A few days later, the Bytec group of Cowpland, St. John, and Tuddenham decided that Dynalogic would lose its autonomous corporate identity and become a division of Bytec. In return for his shares in Dynalogic, Bell would get shares in Bytec. On January 1, 1983, St. John moved from the racquet club into Bell's office. The deposed president's papers were carried out of the executive suite and deposited in a cramped office in the middle of the building. His title as a new employee of Bytec was vice-president, technology. His job would be to evaluate the technological worth of new investment opportunities. He would no longer have any direct responsibility for the Hyperion. The first eighty Hyperions left the plant in January, and St. John and Cowpland decided that the marketing task could be accomplished by means of an advertising campaign in American business and airline magazines. They reserved $1.2 million worth of space in the magazines' May 1983 issues.

Bell, understandably, was angry and dejected at being shunted aside from the Hyperion project. He and St. John had always seemed to work together harmoniously, and St. John was sympathetic if a little puzzled by Bell's resentment. St. John, the college quarterback, believed in team spirit and thought that everyone should agree to do the job he could handle best. "The person who creates a product and gets a company to a certain level is not the kind of person required to manage its growth. Different attributes and a larger team are needed." Bell's new role would focus his talents where they would be most effective, in building Bytec into a major operating company that would eventually follow Mitel in issuing shares to the public. Bell would be Bytec's scout at the frontier of computer technology. "He's going to be our eyes and ears out there," said St. John.

Cowpland, too, admires Bell's engineering skill. "We have a superb technical team there, and Murray's got to take a lot of credit for that." But Cowpland is blunt in his assessment of Bell's performance as a

179

manager. "Murray was pretty weak at marketing. Probably now he'd be OK, but he wasn't learning fast enough. He wanted to spend a fortune on marketing research and consultants, and we felt that was totally unnecessary. It was clear what had to be done, and we thought he should just go ahead and do it."

In Cowpland's mind, what had to be done was simply to hire independent marketing reps to work for commission only and then back them up by placing ads in magazines. "At Mitel we tend to be sceptical about consultants," he says. "We've always found that in a fast-moving industry nobody is an expert unless they're in it. It's pretty hard to observe from the outside because it's moving so damn fast. I really like Murray," Cowpland continues. "But during the period we're talking about, he wasn't a very good CEO. He didn't communicate as much as I like to see. In this kind of business you've got to go 'woomph' and tell everybody everything all of the time and hope that everything comes back to you. Otherwise you make mistakes. He was not that way. I'd tell him things and he wouldn't tell his engineers."

In February emotions seemed to be calming and moves were made to assuage hurt pride. Bell was restored to the front of the Dynalogic building in a bigger, more prestigious office near St. John's. But the Dynalogic sign, which had sat on squat pedestals at the entrance, had been replaced by a new one reading "Bytec." The Dynalogic name was to be expunged; the machine would be known as the Bytec Hyperion. Two months after his shift, Bell outwardly appeared resigned to his new situation. "My job basically is to look at new developments. Look at new computers, tear them apart. But in a sense it's not quite the same. I guess once you've been in the driver's seat – I mean you can have fun doing that, but it's not quite the same."

Carol Bell hoped Murray would settle into his new job and give more time to family life. But she was fatalistic. "He's probably going to start up something different, I guess. I don't look forward to that. I would probably like him to get a job with regular hours – eight to four, something like that. But I have a feeling that's not going to happen."

On Wednesday, March 9, 1983, Bell told the engineers and staff who had developed the Hyperion that he was quitting Bytec to look for a new business project. "Perhaps that's the role of the entrepreneur, to start things up and then move on to something else," he shrugged.

Cowpland genuinely seemed to regret Bell's departure. "Maybe he's learned enough to overcome some of his weaknesses next time." Bell will, according to Cowpland, have the means to convert his dreams into reality, at least if Bytec manages to repeat the Mitel triumph on the stock market. "He's made a lot of money. He's got 300,000 shares of Bytec, which are worth six dollars each. I think they'll go up by a factor of five when Bytec goes public, so his shares will probably be worth about ten million dollars."

Until then, however, in Bell's estimation, his shares are "just a lot of wallpaper." His bitterness at having lost Dynalogic has abated. He still plays racquetball at Cowpland's Queensview club and, in fact, lost fifty pounds during the three months following his departure from Bytec thanks to exercise and diet. Physical renewal was a sign that his attention had turned from resentment to starting over.

By the time the sap was flowing in the sugar bush behind his house in the countryside south of Kanata, Bell was back in his basement, this time surrounded by the best in office wall units, tables, and two new computers, an IBM and the one Hyperion he received as part of his severance settlement. He had just sent away for a Heathkit home robot. "Some people say home robots are today where home computers were five years ago," Bell confided, his eyes agleam with the earnest anticipation of a child awaiting a promised new toy.

Cowpland and St. John, meanwhile, scrambled to make a commercial success of Bell's Hyperion. Unfortunately for them, production of the machine lagged behind their sales plan, causing the expensive springtime ad blitz to pump a dry well. Few Hyperions were available to satisfy the demand created by the advertising. In July, St. John reported a backlog of firm orders worth $25 million for the Hyperion and "soft" orders of at least equal value. Yet only about two thousand machines had been produced by the Ottawa plant, while in Alabama, SCI was just starting to make the Hyperions for the U.S. market. Production costs were straining Bytec's borrowing power, and Cowpland and St. John decided to sell off the most profitable of Bytec's investments – its shares in Comterm, which had doubled in value to $1.5 million in eighteen months.

The sale was hardly an indication of lack of esteem for Comterm. On the contrary, their experience as Comterm board members since the start of 1982 had confirmed the confidence of Cowpland and St. John in the company's president, Laurent Nadeau. "He's a gentleman," says St. John, "and it's always best to do business with a gentleman." In turn, Nadeau was impressed by the Hyperion and saw in it a natural complement to Comterm's line of terminals compatible with IBM's big mainframe computers.

Cautiously, Nadeau and St. John began to moot ways of deepening the relationship between Comterm and Bytec, particularly since both companies were just beginning to feel their way in the American market. Their discussions culminated in mid-summer, 1983, in a surprise decision to merge Bytec with Comterm. If approved by Comterm shareholders, Cowpland would be chairman of the company, and St. John would remain with him in Ottawa as president of its investment division. For Bytec shareholders, the merger would permit a quick conversion of their investments into publicly traded stock and a chance to recover their capital while new money was being raised from the public to finance growth. The manoeuvre would be accomplished through the purchase of Bytec by Comterm, with payment made in the form of Comterm shares, which were listed on the stock exchanges of Montreal and Toronto.

Under the terms of the deal, Comterm's building in Pointe Claire would become the head office of the merged computer company with Nadeau as president – furthering his determination to make a "vallée du silicon" of Montreal. It was also tempting to see in the merger a renewed trust between Quebec and English Canada and hope for a modern, national entente founded on mutual respect and economic good sense. Nadeau is discreet about his politics – governments are important customers of computer companies – but he reflects an attitude general among Quebec businessmen and young adults. Independence has become, for them, an illusory and irrelevant objective destined to fade from significance with the political eclipse of the Parti Québécois's current leadership.

High technology now proffers the lure of individual and social well-being once monopolized by political ideology. And since the essence of high technology is the defiance of time and geography through instant communication, it reduces traditional nationalisms –

both Quebec and Canadian – to folkloric anachronisms. Thus, timid protectionism is decaying as the dominant economic ethos. Taking its place is an exciting, outward-looking quest for intelligent risk and adventure that is closer in spirit to the sturdy optimism of the country's first European settlers than to the trepidation of its economic and political leaders of the past hundred years.

187

188